SCRAPPY ROUGH DRAFT

USE SCIENCE TO STRATEGICALLY
MOTIVATE YOURSELF & FINISH WRITING
YOUR BOOK

DONNA BARKER

THE CREATIVE ACADEMY

ISBNs

978-1-926691-88-6 (Mobi)

978-1-926691-89-3 (ePub)

978-1-926691-90-9 (Softcover)

978-1-926691-91-6 (Hardcover)

978-1-926691-92-3 (Audiobook)

This book is dedicated to 97 writers who participated in the November 2017 beta delivery of Book On Fire. You taught me that real friendships can grow inside virtual communities.

And to Dave, who tolerates me spending more time with my muse than I spend with him when I'm working on my scrappy rough drafts.

CONTENTS

A note about spelling…   vii
The Philosophy of The Creative Academy   ix
How to get the most from this book   xi

1. From shitty first draft to scrappy rough draft   1
2. What are the steps in writing a first draft?   13
3. Universal rules for writing your scrappy rough draft   25
4. What are your beliefs about writers and first drafts?   35
5. The science of self-talk   41
6. Why you'll never create the time to write   49
7. Harnessing the power of "Yes, and…"   55
8. Choosing 'this and that,' not 'this or that'   61
9. Who are you? Who, who? Who, who?   67
10. The science of the inner critic   77
11. Harnessing the power of "Yes…but…"   91
12. Harnessing the power of "…yet"   99
13. Show passion the door and get to know your purpose as a writer   105
14. Goal-setting versus domain and directional planning   113
15. How to develop 'fresh start' behaviours   127
16. If you don't know where/how to start   139
17. You can tell a story 100 ways   143
18. Pick one focus and stick with it   149
19. How to use a carrot as a stick to meet writing targets   157
20. Skulking around the writer's block   161
21. Why it's important to celebrate small wins   171
22. Bringing it together   181

More Creative Academy books   185
Acknowledgments   187
List of resources   189

A note about spelling…

All three of the founding members of The Creative Academy live in Canada, and we made a conscious decision to use Canadian spellings throughout our book series. Because…well…it's who we are, eh?!

A note to our American readers and other friends from around the world… we welcome U in Canada :) Thanks for your willingness to learn new things and play nice with your colourful Canadian neighbours.

While we always appreciate readers letting us know if you find errors in our books, pretty please double check Canadian spellings before you tell us we're wrong!

When we're quoting someone and the quote had American spellings, we left those intact.

xo Donna, Eileen and Crystal

THE PHILOSOPHY OF THE CREATIVE ACADEMY

Unlike many writers, I didn't know I wanted to write when I was still in elementary school. In fact, I became a writer virtually against my will. I always loved the production side of storytelling: I was the editor of our high school yearbook, the production manager of my college newspaper, and in my university communications degree, I focused on producing and editing film. Once in the workforce, although I'd been hired as a project manager, my secret (even to me) ability to write became known and I found myself in an accidental career as a technical ghostwriter.

It wasn't until I was forty years old that I decided I wanted to write a book. And given I'd been called a writer for over a decade, I thought making the leap to writing a story from my heart would be easy. Boy was I wrong.

That's why we started The Creative Academy, an online community that fosters big dreams for writers and provides practical guidance to reach those writing dreams. A space where writers find their peers and build the support networks we all need on our book-writing journeys. The place to go when you need credible people who've been where you are now, to assure you that, "You've got this," especially when you feel you very much don't got this.

This book is hopefully a part of that journey for you and if you aren't already, we hope you'll consider joining us online at The Creative Academy. We're holding a seat for you and can't wait to hear about your book.

HOW TO GET THE MOST FROM
THIS BOOK

In 2014, I took part in a vision-setting workshop. One activity was to find a word that we identified as our core desired feeling. The word that came to my mind and has stuck with me for over five years was not on the suggested list: it was **bungee**. To me, bungee represents my happy place, no matter what activity I'm engaged in. It's that feeling of being grounded and safe but also free to fly out into the world at high speed, knowing that if I don't like what I find, my trip back to home base is available for me.

I wrote this book with my core desired feeling as a guide. You can jump in to a section that sounds interesting, read what's there and see if it resonates, try the activity and see how it feels. That said, I do suggest you read the first two sections, *From shitty first draft to scrappy rough draft* and *What are the steps in writing a first draft?* to best understand the big picture context of the rest of the book. But from there the sections will make just as much sense if you treat this book like an oracle deck, flipping open a page at random and 'bungeeing' out from there.

Each section ends with one or two action-oriented exercises for you to tackle, since changing behaviours and making progress on a goal requires more than simply reading. If you thought this book had answers for you, sorry. What this book has is a solid rationale for asking some good questions that will lead you to your own perfect answers. You need to actually do the work... I know... bait and switch.

Most of these **Your Turn** exercises can be done in a notebook, which I recommend you have at-hand while reading this book. A few exercises are easier to do on a worksheet. When that's the case, I've provided a link to an online download.

So, make sure your harness is comfortable: it's time to jump!

FROM SHITTY FIRST DRAFT TO
SCRAPPY ROUGH DRAFT

"Perfectionism is the voice of the oppressor, the enemy of the people. It will keep you cramped and insane your whole life, and it is the main obstacle between you and a shitty first draft."
~Anne Lamott

Virtually every writer can see our story ideas come to life inside our heads in beautifully composed and communicated scenes. The prose that floats around in our genius idea-brains is poetic and clear. In our mind's eye, the stories we want to share flow from our fingers as effortlessly as eagles riding thermals.

And then, we start to write. And it's hard. The story that has told itself in our head for months or years, decides to hide in dark corners and will not show itself no matter how much we plead and cajole and promise ourselves great rewards once the work is done.

Yes, most of us will get some pages written. For some of us

it will be pages of notes, for others, full scenes or chapters. We write and feel good about our progress. Until we read those words with a critical eye. Sadly, this is the spot where a high majority of first-time authors quit writing.

In 2002, The New York Times ran an article that cited an unnamed study which found that 81% of Americans "feel they have a book in them—and that they should write it." Looking at the most current data available in 2019 from Bowker, the total number of self-published print and ebook titles using American ISBNs was just over one million in 2017.

It sounds like a lot—and it *is* a growing number. But, in a population of 325.7 million in 2017, simple math tells us that only one out of every 325 Americans published a book in 2017. Or, three out of every thousand people, not the 810 per 1,000 who claim to have a book in them they'd like to write.

Of course, that simple math is grossly inaccurate for four reasons:

First, some writers knocked their "write a book" goal off their bucket list in 2016, and some in 2000, and others in 1967… and others will in 2020 and beyond.

Second, that one million ISBNs is only for self-published books. Publishers also use ISBNs so the one million is likely closer to 1.5 million unique numbers.

But, one book title can be assigned several ISBNs since reprints, ebooks, audio books, paperbacks, and hard covers are all given unique numbers.

And then we have the unknown variable of how many authors published more than one book. With the trend toward publishing novellas and "short reads" some authors are able to publish a dozen titles in a year without breaking a sweat.

Despite the impossibility of calculating precisely how many people with books in them actually get them written, we can still conclude one thing: worldwide, millions of dreamer-writers never become published authors.

Thousands of books have been written to help writers become published authors. The majority of those are focused on the craft of writing or the business of being a working (aka earning) author. Significantly fewer focus on the step that comes *before* you have a draft to polish or a manuscript to share with readers.

Of the books I've read and the courses I've taken that address author mindset, virtually all ask the reader to identify the root of their negative self-talk, do exercises to quiet the voices, and generally take quite a *woo woo* approach to conquering those writing demons.

To be clear, I don't dismiss the power of this work and have drawn on much of it in my own writing life and as a coach and course-creator. But sometimes that is just not enough to get to "The End."

Perhaps because my favourite question is, "Why?" and my typical productive procrastination activity is research, I went in search of an answer to what keeps people from finishing important goals. I sought answers from social and neuroscientists to learn what they've figured out our brains are *really* doing when they take us away from our book-writing goals and drop us in front of the next great Netflix binge.

The good news, I learned, is that everything you need to finish your rough draft is inside you. This book is like a flashlight that can help you see into the dark corners where your words have been hiding. I designed the exercises to give you the tools to coax those words from your brain through your fingertips and into grammatically imperfect, typo-laden manuscripts that can be edited into a book you'll be proud to talk about at your next high school reunion.

But, before cracking open the door of the dusty crawlspace where your story is hiding out, I want to talk about the original title I had for this book and the impact of the words we use to think and talk about our writing.

When this book—the one you're reading—was in its own first draft I had it titled "Shitty First Draft" in honour of the advice shared by Anne Lamott in her classic book for writers, *Bird by Bird: Some Instructions on Writing and Life.* Since the expression has become common short-hand for writers who are working on their first drafts, it seemed to make sense. But the more I wrote, the more clear it became that even just as a title, those three words undermined the core message of this book:

No matter how rough your first draft is, it must be honoured.

And "shitty" simply does not communicate that intention.

> **"Perfectionism is the voice of the oppressor, the enemy of the people. It will keep you cramped and insane your whole life, and it is the main obstacle between you and a shitty first draft."** *~Anne Lamott*

I understand why Anne Lamott asked us to think of our first draft as shitty—to give us the space to write without restraint. And for years I used her vernacular to describe my own manuscripts, but I never felt great about calling my work shitty since it triggered this little voice that made me feel like I was a shitty writer. But it was Anne Lamott, for goodness' sake. She knows way more than I do about writing books so, I continued to use the term and —*heavens!*—I even applied it to the first draft manuscripts of my coaching clients.

Until one day a client rebelled. With English as her second language, she interpreted the description literally and understood I was suggesting her first draft should be flushed away.

Of course, that's not how Lamott intended us to interpret her phrasing. But as writers, I believe we can do better. I know we can overthrow the oppressor, Perfectionism, without giving voice to the negative Inner Critic who interprets our words so literally.

The words we use matter

As a writer, you know that the words you use matter.

For instance, when your protagonist faces her unfair boss, the way you describe that scene will leave the reader with a clear understanding of who she is. Although the words 'competitive,' 'forceful,' 'audacious' and 'dynamic' are all synonyms of 'aggressive,' they each draw a slightly different picture of your heroine's character.

In the same way, the descriptive words you choose to describe your work-in-progress, be it your first draft or your tenth revision, matter. Maybe more than you consciously realize.

Why does this matter to you, a writer who may be happy to call your first draft "shitty?" Because our language and our thoughts are woven together; even minor variations in wording can have a profound impact on how we feel about things and also how we remember experiences.

So, if we're all calling our first drafts "shitty," we're both applying a negative judgement to our work-in-progress *and* influencing the way we'll remember the process of writing the first draft.

Do we really want to associate all of those first draft emotions and images with the word "shitty?"

I certainly don't. I suspect you don't, either.

Shitty First Scarf? Shitty First Meatball? Shitty First Orgasm?

Our first time doing anything—knitting a scarf, making meatballs, having sex—is something we know we'll get better at with time and practice and revisions.

We all know that our first efforts will not be our best work. We don't have knitters and cooks and lovers qualifying their first efforts with a universally accepted insult. And yet, many writers seem to proudly don the shitty first draft cloak as if it's an inevitable stage of the writing process.

- But how are we judging our work-in-progress when we call our work shitty?
- How are we judging ourselves as writers?
- When our book is finally done and we're remembering the feelings we had writing our first draft, will we ever want to live through those unpleasant feelings again?

Changing the framing makes a difference

"First draft" as a concept is a neutral thing. It is neither good nor bad. It simply is. But in service of overcoming perfectionism, legions of writers have accepted adding a descriptive word that turns the first draft into something negative.

- What if instead we were to all find the perfect words to describe our own imperfect first draft, words that respect our manuscripts and honour us as writers?
- How much easier might it be to get those first drafts done?

Those were the questions I wondered about. So, I tested them in my community and in workshops at two writers' conferences.

I started by redefining how I think and talk about my own creative non-fiction work-in-progress. For me, I feel great calling it a 'scrappy rough draft.' Now, these words may not resonate with you, but the image that 'scrappy' and 'rough' evoke for me is positive.

Scrappy rough draft feels full of promise and fight and fire. And my work-in-progress needs that. It doesn't need to have a visual of a toilet bowl, it wants a visual of a puppy backed into a corner and launching at the enemy with snarling teeth. That suits the topic of my book, me as a writer, and my personality.

A writer working on a Young Adult story with a shape-shifter as a main character might feel like she's writing a **magical first draft**. Think about what that suggests about the stage of the story. Magic is transformational, magic creates a world of potential, sometimes magic even sparkles. And since the character of this story can transform, it makes it easy (or at least easier) to feel the transformational qualities, the magical qualities, that take place between the first and final drafts.

A memoir writer in one of my workshops decided her work-in-progress was a **faithful first draft**. A picture book author called hers a **silly first draft**. A writer working on a novella about a private eye gave his story the power of a **muscular tough draft**.

Another author now thinks of her first draft as her **stubborn story** since she's been working on it, on and off, for over ten years. In adjusting that one word from "shitty" to "stubborn" she said,

"Now when I think about sitting down to write I have this positive feeling of a story that will not leave me alone until I finish it, as opposed to how I had been feeling, like writing my book was a waste of time."

When Anne Lamott used the word "shitty" to help us remove that mental obstacle of seeking perfection with the first draft, she opened new doors to a healthy creative process for many writers—perhaps millions. But, it turns out, she also created a new obstacle for *some* of us.

Your Turn

Step 1: Figure out your perfect perfection-buster descriptor

Coming up with a new way to describe your work-in-progress can be easy. Answer the following three questions and within a few minutes, you'll be able to flush away that shitty first draft and replace it with a draft that perfectly reflects the beautiful work-in-progress that's captured your imagination.

1. What are some qualities of your genre?

Think about what makes your genre special and see if any of the words that describe it fit how you feel about your first draft.

- If you write mystery, your first draft might be Enigmatic or Puzzling.
- If you write romance your first draft could be Seductive or Lovely.
- If you write non-fiction about historic cities, you could be writing a Gritty first draft.

2. What are the qualities of your protagonist?

Use the same approach when thinking about your main character. The words that describe him or her may be exactly the right way to think about your draft overall.

- Is he a parish priest questioning his faith? How about a Reflective first draft?
- Is she a nine-year-old girl set on becoming a parasitologist? That sounds like a Wormy first draft to me.
- Are they a middle-aged person coming to terms with their gender? That could be a Brave, Unshakable, or Unflinching first draft.

3. What words would you love to have reviewers use when describing your book?

Perhaps the easiest way to think of these words is to have a look at the books and authors you most admire and find words in the reviews or in their book descriptions.

- I adore author Mary Roach and the word that I'd choose to feel a connection to her writing is Outrageous first draft.

- I'm also a fan of AJ Jacobs and to feel like my first draft was leading to a book I'd be proud to know he'd read, I might call it a Gonzo first draft.

Step 2: Pick a word and try it on

The beauty of giving your first draft a name of its own is that you can change it any time you like. It may feel perfect to think of and refer to your manuscript as Scrappy for the first months you're working on it, when it's fighting with you on every page. But then, that might change and your work-in-progress might feel more like an Agreeable first draft once you've tackled the muddled middle.

Here's a list of 204 adjectives to help get you in a descriptive state-of-mind. Maybe your perfect word is here or perhaps this list will help you discover it.

Absurd
Ace
Alluring
Amazing
Argumentative
Astonishing
Astounding
Audacious
Auspicious
Awesome
Barfy
Beautiful
Beguiling
Bewitching
Blessed
Bodacious
Bold
Brassy
Brave
Breathtaking
Bright
Brilliant
Bullish
Capital
Captivating
Charming
Comforting
Committed
Contemptable
Courageous
Cracking
Crummy
Daring
Dashing
Dazzling
Decayed
Deliberate
Delightful
Determined
Dirty
Disjointed
Disorganized
Divine
Dogged
Dreamlike
Dreamy
Earnest
Enchanting
Encouraging
Engaging

Enthralling
Entrancing
Evil
Evolving
Exceptional
Extraordinary
Fabulous
Faint
Fair
Fanciful
Fantastic
Fascinating
Fearless
First-rate
Foetid
Glorious
Golden
Gorgeous
Great
Gritty
Gutsy
Hallowed
Hazy
Heady
Heartening
Heavenly
Heroic
Holy
Hopeful
Hypnotic
Idyllic
Imperfect
Impressive
Inconceivable
Incredible
Indefatigable
Insistent
Intoxicating
Intriguing
Inviting
Irresistible
Lovely
Mad
Magical
Magnetic
Magnificent
Maggoty
Marvelous
Meditative
Mesmeric

Mesmerizing
Mind-blowing
Mind-boggling
Miraculous
Misty
Monumental
Musing
Out-of-this-world
Outstanding
Ovacious
Pensive
Perfunctory
Persevering
Persistent
Pertinacious
Phenomenal
Plucky
Prodigious
Promising
Pugnacious
Purposeful
Radical
Raucous
Rare
Reflective
Remarkable
Repulsive
Resolved
Revered
Revolting
Rough
Rosy
Ruminative
Sacred
Salty
Sanctified
Scrappy
Seductive
Sensational
Shadowy
Single-minded
Singular
Smashing
Soothing
Speculative
Spellbinding
Spiffy
Spirited
Spunky
Staggering

Staunch
Steadfast
Steely
Stellar
Stinky
Stout
Striking
Strong-willed
Stubborn
Stunning
Stupendous
Sublime
Superb
Superficial
Superlative
Surpassing
Stellar
Tenacious
Terrific
Thoughtful
Too-good-to-be-true
Top-notch
Tremendous
Unbelievable
Uncommon
Undaunted
Uneven
Unflinching
Unheard of
Unimaginable
Unique
Unparalleled
Unprecedented
Unrelenting
Unshakeable
Unsystematic
Unthinkable
Untidy
Unusual
Unusually good
Unwavering
Unyielding
Venerated
Vile
Wicked
Wild
Wonderful
Wondrous
Wormy
Wretched

2

WHAT ARE THE STEPS IN WRITING A FIRST DRAFT?

"The reason we struggle with insecurity is because we compare our behind-the-scenes to everyone else's highlight reel." ~Steve Furtik, Tweet, May 10, 2011

With a communications degree majoring in filmmaking, I struggle to become fully engrossed in movies because I "see" the behind-the-scenes. I know every step that a scene went through—from script to filming to foley to final edit —before it became something that had viewers sitting on the edge of their seat or wiping away tears.

Having written, directed and edited my own films, I learned that for every minute of film that made it to my final projects, a dozen minutes or more were swept away from the cutting room floor. And then, from a 10-minute film, perhaps just 30-seconds would be worthy of a highlight reel. I'd write, direct and edit up to 120 minutes of footage for just 30 seconds of gold.

The same is true with books. When we read a published book, we have no idea how many words were written then removed, how many scenes were developed then deleted. We highlight a few passages that speak to us and that's what we remember of the books we love—the highlights. And it's those highlight-worthy passages we believe we *should* be writing as we're writing our own scrappy rough drafts.

Nothing could be further from the truth.

In *The Writer's Book of Hope*, Ralph Keyes has a chapter on inspiration in which he writes about the necessity of rewriting and how he can tell when an author has rushed through that stage too quickly. Here's how he describes the result:

> *"They are soufflé pulled from the oven halfway through the baking by an impatient chef. Their prose is labored, wordy, hard to follow. Run-on sentences dart about. Vague language weighs down the page. Clichés prop up muddled thoughts. The text is flaccid, not tight. Repetitions abound. In other words, they read like an early draft."*

Why do so many of us place such unrealistic expectations on the quality of our first drafts? I wonder if our love of writers' quotes might have contributed to a belief that as long as we put our butts in our chairs, anyone can write a book. One such quote comes immediately to mind:

> *"There is nothing to writing. All you do is sit down at a typewriter and bleed."*

Of course, we all know that Hemingway did not mean it literally. But the combination of words like "nothing to writing" and "all you do" with a visual of an open wound evokes a particular feeling of, "how hard can it be?" and a process that has all of two steps: 1) cut your arm 2) let the blood drip.

I'd have fewer problems with this metaphor if it included some harder steps, like 1) find a blade (identify your story), 2) realize it's too dull to break skin (appreciate that there are holes in the story idea), 3) look for something to sharpen the blade (do some research), and so on.

Writing is a circular process, not a linear action

Dr. Donald Murray has been called 'America's Greatest Writing Teacher.' I'm somewhat of an evangelist for the way he describes the writing process.

In an article in 1972, he wrote,

> *"The writing process itself can be divided into three stages: prewriting, writing, and rewriting. The amount of time a writer spends in each stage depends on his personality, his work habits, his maturity as a craftsman, and the challenge of what he is trying to say. It is not a rigid lock-step process, but most writers most of the time pass through these three stages."*

Dr. Murray even broke down the time a writer should spend working at each of the three stages: 85 percent on prewriting, one percent on writing, and 14 percent rewriting. Now, keep in mind he was teaching university students who were struggling with writing theses, not writers like you and I, working on novels and memoirs and business-related books.

While 85 percent of one's time at the prewriting stage is likely normal for a graduate student working on a research-based thesis, for most novelists, memoirists, and creative non-fiction writers this might seem like overkill. But when you consider what's included in the prewriting stage the number seems less outrageous.

The point in sharing these categories is to help you recognize and acknowledge all the work you do in service of writing your scrappy rough draft that is not technically writing words in the actual manuscript. We sometimes get hung up on this idea that we're only writing our book when we're *actually* writing. In reality, most writers are *working on* their books for far more hours than the time it takes to put first draft words on a page.

Acknowledging this time is important since it can help us more clearly see the depth of commitment we've made to our stories, even if we're not producing words as quickly as we think we should. Or, the words are not as polished as we want them to be. As you read these categories give yourself credit for work done.

Prewriting includes…

Reading

Reading books in the genre you're writing helps you understand the tropes, structure and reader's expectations of those kinds of stories. This is critical prewriting time. I speak from embarrassing, first-hand experience that writing and editing a 110,000-word manuscript in a genre you don't know and love will only end in tears—and likely, with all those words being placed "under the bed" to live and die.

This reading can also include reviewing notes you've written over the years, if this is an idea you've lived with for a while. It's heartening to be reminded of the ideas you'd jotted down and forgotten, or to read a draft of a scene and see that sure, it needs some massaging but, darn it all, there's good stuff there.

Talking to people about your story

Articulating the story that lives in your head to friends, family, colleagues, other writers and people you meet on public transit is another prewriting step you might spend time on. Talking about your characters (if you're writing fiction), your life experience (if memoir), or lessons learned (if a business book), and getting feedback from people before you start writing can make the blood—your words —flow more easily. For some writers.

For others, this is a part of prewriting to avoid at all costs. The point is that if you *are* the kind of writer who talks about your work-in-progress, that time counts toward your book-writing time. If it's important to you, it's important to acknowledge.

Research

As a dominantly non-fiction writer, I can easily spend 85 percent of writing time here. I know I've hit on a topic that I can go the distance with when I find it hard to stop researching and move on to the writing. Depending on what your book is about, your research may be limited to figuring out appropriate names for your main characters, learning about 19th Century sea-faring women, or walking along the Kelso Dunes in the Mojave Desert.

Also, even after you've *technically* moved into the writing stage, there are dozens of reasons for you to come back to the pre-writing stage. For instance, you might have to stop writing to interview your main characters, to better understand their motivations when they hit a tricky scene. (If this happens to you, Eileen Cook's book *Build Better Characters* would be a good use of a bit more of your pre-writing time.)

Sketching out your book or story idea

Knowing where you sit on the Plotter / Plantser / Pantser continuum can give you a bit more confidence in your writing process, especially if other writers suggest you might be "doing it wrong" since you're not using their tried and true approach to getting your scrappy rough draft written.

A plotter will create an outline for how the story or book unfolds, from Act 1, Scene 1 through to The End. The outline may be dozens of detailed pages, a series of notecards or anything in between. It could include character backstories, detailed location descriptions, collages of photographs and even music playlists to help set the tone of the book. Some plotters spend weeks or months in this prewriting stage.

At the other end of the spectrum are pantsers, people who write by the seat-of-their-pants without worrying where the story is going when they first start. They have a broad idea, maybe a couple of characters in mind with a goal or a good conflict and they let those characters tell the story the way it comes to them.

And the planster is a hybrid who approaches their manuscript with more than just a vague idea, but less than an actual outline. They have a good idea about their story but leave a lot of room for their imagination to highjack it once they get writing.

Writing includes...

Putting words on the page

Of course, you can be putting words on the page while you're in the prewriting stage and will absolutely be putting new words on the page when you're in the first of perhaps several trips into the rewriting stage. The process of writing your scrappy rough draft is not linear.

Staring out the window

Or, at a wall. Or perhaps removing fingers from keyboard and patting a furry friend for several minutes while your mind wanders, ponders, and figures out what terrible situation to put your poor protagonist into next. This is why it can be helpful to think of the way your book is coming to life as 'working' on it, not just 'writing' it, since thinking when your fingers aren't moving across a keyboard counts as writing time.

Rewriting includes...

Revising and editing and revising some more

This last part of the process is one that we're not going to spend much time on because writing your scrappy rough draft is easiest to do if you take your editor's cap, put it in a nice hatbox and place it in the farthest corner on the highest shelf in your closet. Your goal with your first draft is to get the story out and onto the page without judgement. And if you've done some or all of the work in the prewriting stage, you can feel confident that your scrappy rough draft will stand a fighting chance of avoiding the under-the-bed purgatory.

Give yourself credit for time-served

Before I launched the *Book on Fire* course, I asked applicants to answer some questions about their writing, so I could understand who was applying and also how best to help them. One of the questions I asked was simply, "How long have you been working on your book?"

Respondents were offered five choices: a) under 1 year b) 1 to 3 years c) 3 to 5 years d) 5 to 10 years e) over 10 years.

Before you read what the statistics showed, do two things: answer the question for yourself and guess where the majority of the 204 respondents (200 women and 4 men) landed.

	10%	20%	30%	40%	50%	
5.4%	■					Under one year
15.2%	■■					Between 1 and 3 years
30.4%	■■■					Between 3 and 5 years
14.2%	■■					Between 5 and 10 years
34.8%	■■■■					Over 10 years

I hope that your takeaway from this graph is that if you've been working on your book—in any of the three stages—for five years or longer that you are in the normal range for a first book.

And, if you're at the upper end of the "how long/desire to write" spectrum, embrace this as great news. The story has ripened through all that prewriting and your desire has stuck with you for years. It's time to accept that it will be with you until the day you die unless you get that story told. You're ready.

Now all you need is some accountability to help ensure you dedicate the time to the work, some encouragement to keep you moving forward when you feel stuck, and a community of cheerleaders to help you see that you are a writer, that your story does matter, and that your scrappy rough draft is just the first important step towards finishing your book.

Why don't we compare keystrokes to (hobbyist) rocket science?

Think about any other hobby you might decide to pick up —playing an instrument, painting, quilting, hot-rodding an old car—you wouldn't sit down and expect to play Chopin, paint a Picasso, sew like Marianne Fons or chop a '64 Chevy as well as Boyd Coddington would you?

And yet, when we write, we have outrageous expectations on our abilities. I believe part of the problem is that since we read voraciously, have a prodigious vocabulary and know how to type, we set unreasonable expectations on our first drafts. Because, what else do you need to write a book? Ha!

Well, even though I have fingers and sheet music and a piano (and a grandmother who played beautifully and tried for years to teach me) the best I can play is The Celebrated Chop Waltz, more commonly known as Chopsticks.

But my son, who has had no formal training, can sit down at a piano and within a day be playing a keyboard version of his favourite pop song. Why is this? Sure, he might have some natural talent but most of what makes him succeed is his commitment and not having any fear of being judged as he learns the song.

He plays scrappy combinations of sounds for the first two

hours with so many mistakes I can't recognize the song. But then the chords start to make sense to me, and I can hear what he's trying to play. And after another hour or two, he's able to sing along. After a week of practice, that song is ready to be played on his school piano in the common room, where kids can hear—and judge.

Shortly before my dad died, he had his old accordion tuned so he could gift it to my son. Dad's one request was that Liam learn to play the Chicken Song from *The Lawrence Welk Show*. Liam set to the task quickly and with purpose: he knew he had a limited time to learn the song. Of course, Liam succeeded.

Without that purpose, sad as it was, I am certain Liam would have received the gift graciously but not learned to play anything on that 1950s accordion. Not at age 18 at least.

And that, conveniently, leads us right back to you and your book or story.

Your Turn

If your book or story has been on your mind for more than a couple of years, there's a reason it's not leaving you alone. That story has a purpose. Make an inventory of all the work you've already done on, for, and in service of that story.

If you have scraps of paper with notes about your book scattered around your home, gather them up and put them into a binder so you have them all in one place for easy reference.

If your notes are already in one place but hand-written, start typing them into a document.

If you don't have notes, grab a pen and some paper and start scribbling. Or a get some flip-chart paper and create a story timeline or some kind of graphic representation of your idea.

If you're already into the writing stage and have a document with words (yay, you!), open it within the next 24 hours and reread what you've written. Resist the urge to edit, just catch up with where you are right now.

If you've been writing more recently, open that document (or notebook if you write by hand) within the next 24 hours and write some more.

Basically, no matter how little or much you've done, take some time in the next day to make a concrete move forward with your story.

3

UNIVERSAL RULES FOR WRITING YOUR SCRAPPY ROUGH DRAFT

"We are what we repeatedly do. Excellence, then, is not an act, but a habit." ~Aristotle

Over a decade ago, an editor working on my first manuscript—a story that I will never publish—suggested I read Stephen King's *On Writing*. So, I did. The only thing I specifically remember (aside from his story about how his wife threatened to leave him if he didn't sober up) was that he writes 365 days a year. He writes on his birthday. He writes on Christmas day.

I bet you knew that even if you've never read *On Writing*. Hundreds of people quote King on this factoid about his process as though this is the *only way to be a real writer*, that if you're not following in the creepy footsteps of the King of Horror, you don't deserve to call yourself 'A Writer.'

From the beginning I've poo-poo'd this belief since a) I am a real writer and b) I have spent most of my life as a binge writer who does not even write every week, let alone every day, on my non-work projects and c) I am a real writer, dammit. But in dismissing the *Stephen King Rule for Being a Real Writer*, I also inadvertently dismissed the value of having a writing habit. I believed that since I didn't have any predictable habits, and I was still producing drafts and completing writing projects, that my habit-less approach was working just fine for me.

Once I started to research beyond the anecdotal and quotable writing habits of famous authors, to see if there was any science behind this love affair with daily writing, I was surprised to find that Mr. Spooky Pants is actually onto something important. It's not about writing for four or six hours every day, which most of us couldn't do even if we wanted to since... day jobs. Kids. Eight hours of beauty rest.

Not to mention that demanding an untrained brain and butt to sit and write for even an hour if they're not used to the act is like asking someone who rarely walks farther than across the grocery store parking lot to run a marathon. Your mind can desire this all it wants but the odds of making that happen are virtually zero—until you build your stamina which requires having a routine.

Routines and habits make achieving big goals easier. It's a fact.

Donald Murray, "America's Greatest Writing Teacher," has ten habits that he honed over his fifty years as a working journalist, published poet, professor in a graduate program, and as the author of a dozen books including several on the craft of writing. In case you're curious, his own ten habits are:

- Awareness
- Reacting
- Connecting
- Rehearsal
- Disloyalty
- Drafting
- Ease
- Velocity
- Revision
- Completion

Dr. Murray shares details about each of his habits in his article "A Writer's Habits" which appears in the book *Conversations About Writing: Eavesdropping, inkshedding and joining in* but the details are not really that important. The only habits that matter are the ones that will work for *you*.

Dr. Murray's habits work for him. Mr. King's habits work for him. My habits work for me. And your habits will work for you. *All* you have to do is work on your scrappy rough draft enough to recognize your own patterns. And then make the good and productive patterns a habit.

If you're in the stage of the process where the only habit you can recognize is one of resistance, that's okay. This does not give you permission to throw your arms into the air and declare with great drama (since you are a creative soul) that "I'll *never* get this book written. My only habit is breaking my promise to myself that I'll work on my story at least once a week."

Embedded in that action of thinking about (and the non-action of writing) you'll likely find several habits that move you, quite predictably, from the thought, "I'll work on my book on Saturday at 10 AM for half an hour," to the reality of Saturday morning and your sudden deepest desire to apply Marie Kondo's life-changing magic to tidy up your sock and underwear drawer. Now I'm as delighted as the next person to have my undies folded and my socks settled in a relaxed position, but not at the expense of delaying the completion of my book for one more unnecessary day.

In Chapter 10, **The science of the inner critic** you'll learn about why procrastination isn't (necessarily) a writing sin and how you can use your non-writing time to count as legitimate authoring time, but for now I'm asking you to believe one thing:

> **All the time you've spent not typing words of the story you've been wanting to write, trying to write—whether it be over months or years or even decades—had value.**

There is no reason to beat yourself up over time that you spent fertilizing the ground for this moment. Whether you once judged the non-writing time as good or bad is irrelevant as long as you can see that your experience as a writer who wasn't writing (or not writing as much or as often as you'd have liked to have been writing) has created a habit for you. It may have been conscious or subconscious and, again, what it *was* doesn't matter. Right now it's time to make your writing habit both conscious and clear because you can use that to create a new set of habits to propel you along your own unique path to publication.

In *Writing Down the Bones: Freeing the Writer Within*, Natalie Goldberg's all-time best-selling handbook for writers, she shares her seven Rules for Writing Practice. A few of these need a little more explanation, which I will leave to Ms. Goldberg (buy her book!), but these rules have been credited with having changed the way writing is taught in American schools, so I'd be remiss not to mention them in a chapter called **Universal rules for writing your scrappy rough draft**.

Goldberg's rules are:

- Keep your hand moving
- Lose control
- Don't think
- Don't worry about spelling, punctuation or grammar
- You are free to write the worst junk in the world
- Go for the jugular
- Be specific

Pamela De Barres also shared some rules for writers in *Let It Bleed: How to Write a Rockin' Memoir*.

DeBarres' rules refer specifically to how she wants participants in her memoir-writing courses to approach the assignments. They are reminiscent of Goldberg's rules but have one important difference which is why I want to highlight them. DeBarres' rules are:

- Don't lift your pen off the paper or your fingers from the keyboard
- Don't hold back
- Don't think (the most important)
- Don't second-guess what you've just written or reread every sentence
- Don't cross-out or erase
- Don't censor or judge yourself

I find negatively phrased rules a challenge. It comes from something I learned over two decades ago when my son started to walk and explore the world on his own.

If I said, "Don't touch the lamp," he would look at the lamp and then move toward it as if commanded by God himself to touch it. If I cautioned him to be careful when he was running, wobbly around the house, by saying, "Don't bump into the corner of the table," *Bam!* He'd hit the table. If I wanted him to eat some fruit, all I had to say was, "Don't eat that apple," and it would be in his mouth before I could hide the chocolate bar sitting on the counter beside it.

What the heck? My child wasn't a hellion who delighted in disobeying us. In fact, of all the kids I knew, he was the easiest. So, what was going on?

It turns out that he was doing exactly what his brain or imagination saw me asking him to do because we don't see negatives in our mind's eye. What we see is the action— touch the lamp, bump the table, eat the fruit. Then we have to use a different part of our brain to apply the negative.

The first interpretation is immediate and unconscious. The

"don't" requires thinking and takes longer. And science backs up my belief that my boy wasn't being a brat, he was simply acting in the way he saw my command play out in his head.

Because of this, I believe that Goldberg's rules, most of which are stated in the positive, are stronger and more effective than DeBarres'.

But what about the rule both Goldberg and DeBarres express in the negative: Don't think. Could that rule be stated in the positive? When I consider what happens when I stop thinking as I write, the positive expression of that action for me could be:

Put your ego in the backseat, or

Give your inspiration full control of your writing time.

You may "see" a different way to turn the negatively stated rule into one or more positive statements such as "write your story as you feel it," or "write for yourself knowing that nobody will ever have to read this."

Your Turn

Exercise 1: My positive rules

Think about all the rules you've been told you need to follow to be a "real writer" and get your book written.

Write down the rules that come to mind easily since those

are likely the ones that resonate most deeply with you—either in a positive, "I believe that" way or in the way I reacted to Stephen King's rule, with a *"Pshht! That doesn't apply to me."*

Once you have all the rules you can think of—rules that you've likely been ignoring or feeling bad about breaking—cross them out. Doodle on top of them. Do something to express that you will no longer feel bad about having broken those rules.

Now, set your timer and free write for fifteen minutes in response to this statement:

> *The only rules I need to follow, or habits I need to develop, to finish my scrappy rough draft are...*

When your timer goes off, circle the nuggets that resonate, and can be written as short, positively expressed statements.

My own rule is very simple and allows me to have micro-successes every day—which you'll learn is a critical element to finishing your scrappy rough draft—and it is:

> You will make progress on your work-in-progress every day.

In Chapter 5, **The science of self-talk**, I explain why that statement is written in the second person, not the first person.

Exercise 2: My writing process examined

This is not a theoretical challenge that you simply read and either think has the potential to be helpful or is silly. This is a call-to-action to your Inner Author to take one step toward changing an old habit so you can get your scrappy rough draft finished.

1. Open your calendar.

2. Identify a day, three to five days from now, where you can see that you have a 15-minute block of time that you could spend working on your book. Don't make it tomorrow or the next day!

3. Schedule one 15-minute block with these exact words: **Write My Book**.

4. Find a small notebook that you can (and will) carry with you from now until the day and time of your writing date.

5. Each time you think about your book, make a note about that experience. You may write ideas about the story. Or not. You may have feelings about the thought of sitting down to write. Or not. You may hear the voice of your inner critic saying unkind things about you or your story or this process. Or not.

You may hear a conversation—in real life or on a television show—that you think would be exactly what your protagonist might say in a similar situation. You may read a passage in a novel that inspires you or a passage that makes you think, "I can write better than that." Whatever thoughts you have that you can connect to your own book, jot down a note about them. Be as specific as time allows.

6. When your scheduled writing time arrives, set your timer for fifteen minutes, sit down and do what comes naturally to you. If that's writing, write. If that's staring out the window and wondering what you can write about, stare. If it's reading some of what you've already written, read. Do research. Surf social media. Whatever it is that you feel compelled to do at the time you've intentionally set aside to write, do that thing with no judgment or guilt.

You're in a process and all you need to do is observe what happens.

And then…

7. As soon as possible after your fifteen minutes of writing time has elapsed, write down what happened when you sat down to write, in as much detail as you can. What did you do? What did you feel emotionally? How did you physically feel? What were you thinking? What were you thinking, feeling and doing related to your book in the days between scheduling the writing time and actually putting butt-in-chair?

8. Once you've completed this process, find another date in your calendar where you can spend at least fifteen minutes on your book. But this time schedule yourself to: **Work On My Book**.

You do not want to use the word "write" this time.

9. Go through Stages 1 through 7 again with this new way of framing the time you spend working on your scrappy rough draft. See if it feels any different.

4

WHAT ARE YOUR BELIEFS ABOUT WRITERS AND FIRST DRAFTS?

"A belief is just a thought you keep thinking." ~*Abraham Hicks*

I suspect you've had the following experience: you're away from home in an unfamiliar place and you get hungry. You see two restaurants—one is a chain you know well and one is a place you've never heard of before. Which one will you eat at?

If you're like most people, you'll choose the familiar restaurant *even if you know you don't really like the food.*

This psychological phenomenon is called the **mere exposure effect** and it impacts us in all areas of our life. What it describes is our tendency to develop preferences for things merely because we are familiar with them. Of course, there are areas of our life where this comes in handy, which any parent of a tantrum-throwing toddler will understand. (For non-parents, I'm suggesting that the mere exposure effect is why parents seem to have a superhuman patience with that inhuman child.)

The mere exposure effect is why product and service advertisers invest so much in making sure what they have to sell is put in front of us as often as possible and why Facebook ads are an investment many authors and online entrepreneurs feel confident spending their money on.

Researchers have shown that the mere exposure effect applies to virtually all areas in our life where we make decisions based on perceptions. This includes everything from choosing to attend a certain school to investing in specific stocks, to both developing strong relationships with people and the opposite, reinforcing our negative feelings about people whom we, on first impression, didn't like.

So, how does this relate to your scrappy rough draft?

Think about all the feelings that you have connected to what it means to be a writer and how those feelings are impacting how you feel about your work-in-progress. Some of those feelings are likely operating from the space of the mere exposure effect.

For instance, everyone *knows* that "real writers" are created in the likeness of Stephen King. How many times have you read or heard about his writing habit (write every day, write with the metaphorical door closed), and been told that this is the only way to be a writer? If you've read writing craft books and blogs, my guess is dozens of times—enough times to have placed that information in the "it must be true" column of our What

We Believe About Writing and Being a Writer part of our brain.

The mere exposure effect is tightly tied to another psychological phenomenon called the **illusory truth effect** which is our tendency to believe information to be correct after repeated exposure. Researchers have found that when deciding if something is true or not, people rely on two conditions: 1) whether the information is in line with what they already know, understand and have experienced and 2) whether the information feels familiar. And, in cases where what you know from experience is in conflict with what's been repeated ad nauseam, guess which one will override? Familiarity has been shown in many studies to override rationality.

So, back to getting your scrappy rough draft written. You're very likely facing a double whammy of both having had the experience of it being challenging to sit down and write (which leads your inner critic to nod its head and remind you that it's been telling you're not really a writer ever since you had this crazy idea to write a book) and the familiarity of author-after-author saying that any writer worth their words follows a writing schedule that Ebenezer Scrooge would give you full marks for adopting.

Within this context, how can you figure out what the truth is about being a writer and getting your own scrappy rough draft written?

The easiest way is to test all the assumptions that you have about writers and writing— assumptions that are very likely false that have been planted in your belief system by mere (over) exposure. Easy as that.

(And, next time you're out and about and get hungry, remember these psychological phenomena and choose the restaurant you've never been to before. You may be delighted with that new experience).

Your Turn

In this exercise you'll be testing your assumptions about writing, being a writer, and how polished your pre-edited writing should be. You'll start by answering some questions and writing what you "know" to be true. Then, you'll analyze those assumptions to see if you can identify where the feeling of the truth of the statement comes from. And finally, for all the beliefs that you decide are truths (for instance, "all writers write"), you'll try to find one example of a situation where that truth has been proven to be flexible (for instance, some writers dictate their first draft).

Step 1

Give yourself 20 seconds for each question—no more. Set a timer to help you. Leave space beside or below each answer for the Part 2 portion of the exercise.

- When you think of the kind of writer you'd like to be, who pops to mind?
- What does it takes to be a writer?
- What do you need *to do* to be a writer?

- What do you believe about writers in general? What words come to mind?
- How good should a first draft be?
- What do you believe about authors who make a living from their writing?
- What traits do successful writers have in common?

Step 2

Take your time to answer the following question for each of the answers you wrote down in Part 1 (except for the first one about which authors you imagined).

- Where could that belief have come from?

Step 3

Look at each pair of questions and answers and decide what you choose to believe instead.

- First, determine, is your belief a truth?
- If not, what do you choose to believe instead?

5

THE SCIENCE OF SELF-TALK

"It's not what you say out of your mouth that determines your life, it's what you whisper to yourself that has the most power!"
~Robert T. Kiyosaki

How many times have you read a self-help guru who suggests that one of the steps to achieving a big goal is to write positive affirmations, to visualize yourself as the person you're trying to become? Dozens. Hundreds. Uncountable times if you're in an aspirational mindset stage of life.

And how many times have you dutifully followed the directions and written your affirmations, just like they recommend—

- I am a writer.
- The story I'm telling has value.

- I am the best and only person who can tell this story in this way.
- I am becoming a better writer every day.
- I will write today and every day.
- I am stronger than rejection.
- I believe in myself and in my story.

—only to fail, fail again and finally decide that positive affirmations and visualizations just don't work for you?

Before you cancel your dream of becoming an author and close the door for good on all that affirmation and visualization talk, give me five minutes to share some science that could help you write your perfect aspirational statement to achieve your audacious writing goals.

First person vs second person affirmations

Ninety-six percent of adults (and one infamous Hobbit) speak to themselves, something social science researchers call "self-talk." And although most of us use both the first person ("I") and second person ("you") when giving ourselves pep-talks, not until very recently did a group of researchers decide to differentiate between first person and second person self-talk.

Lots of research has been done on why we talk to ourselves and the impact that can have on our mindset, productivity and so on. But it wasn't until 2014 that the difference between saying, "I am a writer," and "you are a writer" was studied in any detail.

In "The inner speech of behavioral regulation: Intentions

and task performance strengthen when you talk to yourself as a You" researchers found that the "person" we choose with our self-talk has an impact on our success.

While most of the affirmation exercises I've seen recommend writing first person "I" statements, the research clearly shows that in situations that challenge our self-control and self-regulation—like putting your butt in your chair and words on the page—use of the second person pronoun is much more effective. For instance,

- You are committed to your writing.
- You need to stay focused. You can do it.
- You can make this deadline.

One of the reasons it's believed this approach works is due to socialization, the fact that we become used to responding to directions from people who have authority over us—parents, teachers, bosses. So, when we call on our inner "You," that second person inner voice has more power over us than our inner "I" who we're pretty comfortable ignoring.

First person vs third person visualizations

There's another way to use "you" when creating motivational statements. The "You' of visualizing an outsider's perspective to your actions can also have a positive influence on our follow-through with commitments.

In a study done about voter behaviour during the 2004 US

election, researchers Lisa Libby et al gave research participants one of two visualizations to perform:

1. You should picture doing the action from a **first person** visual perspective. With the first person visual perspective **you see the event** as you would have, if the event were actually taking place. That is, **you are looking out at your surroundings through your own eyes**.

2. You should picture doing the action from a **third person** visual perspective. With the third person visual perspective you see the event from the visual perspective **an observer would have** if the event were actually taking place. That is, **you see yourself in the image, as well as your surroundings**.

Participants were also asked to do a series of other tasks related to the visualization. And the results were conclusive:

"Picturing voting from the third person perspective caused subjects to adopt a stronger pro-voting mind-set correspondent with the imagined behaviour.

Further, this effect on self-perception carried over to behaviour, causing subjects who were instructed to picture voting from the third person perspective to be significantly more likely to vote in the election."

This research supports what M.D. Storms found in a 1973 study, "that actions are perceived to be more a function of the actor's character when viewed from an observer's perspective than when viewed from the actor's perspective."

It would appear that seeing oneself as the type of person who would engage in a desired behaviour increases the likelihood of engaging in that behaviour. Do you know if, as a writer at this stage of your writing career, you would respond best to first person or second person affirmations or third person visualizations?

Generally speaking, researchers have found that:

First person affirmations work best when:

- you generally have positive feelings about the activity you're undertaking or the goal you're trying to achieve;
- you're trying to create emotions and feelings.

Second person affirmations work best when:

- you need to distance yourself from negative feelings about a task or a goal;
- you need to strengthen performance, attitudes and behavioural intentions;
- you're engaging in an action or a difficult challenge that requires self-regulation and self-control;
- you need to adopt a broader perspective.

Third person visualizations work best when:

- you need to adjust your self-concept to match a desired behaviour.

***

Your Turn

Not sure what you need right now? Try this exercise.

Exercise 1: First person

Set your timer for two minutes and free-write in the first person voice (I) exactly **what you're thinking, hearing, feeling, believing** about the quality of your writing, your writing habits, etc.

Exercise 2: Second person

Now, imagine you're inside your own head looking at yourself. Set your timer for two minutes and free-write in the close second person voice (you) exactly **what you need to do** to become the writer you aspire to be. Focus on behaviours and actions.

Exercise 3: Third person

Now, imagine you're a distant observer of yourself or that a writer you respect is pointing their finger at you and speaking. Set your timer for two minutes and free-write in the third person (also called distant second person voice) (you) **about the kind of person** who is the kind of writer you aspire to be. Focus on attitudes and values.

Exercise 4: Review the three exercises

Which affirmation or visualization approach do you intuitively feel or know will be the most useful to you right now?

Write down an affirmation or imagine a visualization that matches your need.

6

WHY YOU'LL NEVER CREATE THE TIME TO WRITE

"If you find yourself blaming your lack of 'productivity tools'—an Orwellian euphemism for 'high-tech procrastination devices'—remember the inkwell and typewriter. ~Paul J. Silvia

As a writer who has spent most of my career decoding technical language and making it understandable to regular people, I have a thing for using the right words. I'm not hung up on always finding the *best* words, but they do have to mean what I want them to.

So, yeah, I can be picky and drive the people in my life a bit mad with questions like, "When you say, *That driver is an idiot*, do you mean that they are driving badly, or dangerously, or just that they annoyed you?" (And I never ask when I'm a passenger since a) I can extrapolate having seen the situation and b) ninety percent of the time that I'm a passenger we're on a highway in the middle of nowhere; it would be lousy place to have to hitch a ride.)

And now I'm going to risk being figuratively thrown from your moving vehicle by suggesting that if you've ever said that you can't "*find* the time" or "*make* the time" to write, that you're both 100% right and 100% wrong.

Nobody, except perhaps Hermione Granger in *The Prisoner of Azkaban*, can "make time." Nor is time something we can "find," like a house-key that fell between the cushions on the couch. Yet this is the language we use when we're explaining (usually to ourselves) why we haven't sat down to work on our books.

But we don't use this language of finding or making time when it comes to other areas of life. It's a rare employee who will tell their boss that they just couldn't *find* the time to come to work or *make* the time to do the tasks that they get a paycheque to perform. When an activity is important —like showing up for work and doing our job—we *schedule* the time. We know that we'll wake up at 6:00, spend an hour getting ready, another hour commuting and be in our workspace, perhaps bleary-eyed and cranky, at 8:00.

When you're at the scrappy rough draft stage, the belief that you don't have time to work on your book is, for most people, simply an excuse not to begin taking the risks that accompany starting to write a book.

If I'm honest with myself, I can identify the reasons I won't schedule time to write even when I know I have to protect that time in order to have a finished manuscript to edit. My reasons are the same as virtually every writer I've ever met.

I'm afraid that what I'm thinking about won't be as smart or funny or helpful or brilliant once I've written it down.

I'm worried that I'll get started and within 10,000 words be bored with my story or my characters or my topic.

I'm concerned that anything I want to say has all been said before, and by authors who are more experienced than I am, better writers than me, and have a higher education than my lowly Bachelor of Arts degree.

Somewhere in my mind I carry a false belief that if I was really meant to write this book, the focus and flow would be easy.

And that is a problem since the thoughts we think and reflect back to ourselves become our reality. It's as true with how we feel about our ability to achieve a goal as it is the amount of time we have to work on that goal. If you think about other writers who have successfully completed their scrappy rough draft and had the same—or similar—pressures on their time as you have, it becomes easy to see how our language creates our reality.

On priming your world to include writing

Let's say Adam and Eve both decided to write books. Both had kids to care for, a full-time job, and a schedule that, at the moment the decision to write was made, didn't leave a lot of wiggle room for writing.

Each day Adam wakes up and tells himself he doesn't have time to work on his book. Eve wakes up and tells herself that she's going to schedule time in her busy day to work on her book. She may or may not manage to get words done that day—or even for a few weeks—but each day she wakes up she tells herself that she has time to write, she simply has to schedule it. Adam on the other hand is still telling himself he doesn't have time.

Fast forward a few weeks or even months, Adam's probably stopped thinking about that book idea he had, but Eve has made some progress on her scrappy rough draft because she primed her world to make it possible by using language that affirmed her ability to schedule her time and her days.

On Scheduling time

Robert Boice is a PhD in psychology who spent much of his career studying and helping university faculty become more effective writers. His research proves something that I wasn't thrilled to learn, being a lifetime advocate of binge-writing: it is neither as productive nor does it produce as many creative ideas as scheduling time to write and sticking to your schedule. Darn.

When Boice was doing his research in the 1980s and 90s, he was at the forefront of a new understanding about the connection between productivity and creativity. The traditional belief at that time was that creativity had to be spontaneous and internally motivated. This was perhaps a step better than the preceding era when the traditional belief was that creativity had to fuelled by alcohol and drugs. And the way Boice defined "productivity" sends a chill down my binge-writing spine: "habitual, and if necessary, forced writing."

If it's not clear how this applies to getting your scrappy rough draft done, I'll use my most concise words: schedule time to work on your book on your daily calendar and then… sit down and do the work.

Your Turn

In 2018, I hired a business coach to help me become more focused on all the bits and pieces of being a working writer. The first thing she had me do was write down every single thing I did in a day, in 15-minute increments, for seven days. At first it was painful, but after just three days I could see why I felt like I was spinning my wheels even though I was at my desk, working, at least eight hours a day.

If you're not sure you have time to set aside to work on your book, this exercise will very likely prove otherwise. You can create your own spreadsheet or **download one from our creativeacademyforwriters.com/resources page.**

Keep the tracking sheet near you all day and every time you change activities, make a note of what you've started doing and when. I suspect what you notice will be fascinating—and when you see how you actually spend your time in a typical day, likely empowering.

7

HARNESSING THE POWER OF "YES, AND..."

"The simple fact of sitting down to write day after day is what makes writers productive." ~Ralph Keyes

Have you read the book or seen the movie called *The Yes Man*? The premise is that if we say "Yes," to everything presented to us, we'll live a more interesting and fulfilling life. Of course, even without knowing the story, it's easy to see how this can backfire.

As a writer, there are many places where we *believe* we have to learn to say, "No." But saying "No" can feel bad and the last thing we want to do is attach a negative feeling to our writing.

For instance, you've promised yourself that you'll work on your book on Wednesday evening. You put it in your calendar, and you made the arrangements that needed to be made to make sure your family commitments were being covered by someone else. Good for you.

But then, you get a call from a person you care about. She's in crisis. On Wednesday evening at exactly the time you've committed to your book. What do you do?

You have to choose whether you'll say "No" to yourself or "No" to your friend. At least, that's what most of us believe and how we respond, by choosing one commitment over the other. But what if you could say "Yes" to both? Why can't you?

We can take a lesson from improv actors who are never allowed to say "No" to a new direction in their skits. What they say is "Yes, and…" which allows them to incorporate the new idea without totally abandoning the direction they were headed before the twist.

To be able to act from a "Yes, and…" place, we sometimes need to reframe the two (or more) competing options for our time. For instance, if Sally calls and says, "Oh, my gracious. I don't know what to do. I'm being downsized and won't have a job this time next week. I need someone to talk me down."

You look at your open manuscript. You've juggled all the balls to be able to schedule this time for your book. It wasn't easy. And now your friend needs you. You can't say that you just can't get away since… the only thing keeping you at your desk would be your decision to prioritize your own, selfish desire over your friend's immediate need. Your book has waited this long, what's another day, week, or month? It'll still be there when you're able to schedule that block of time again.

So, you say, "I'm here for you," and you spend the next sixty minutes helping your friend.

In a sense, what you've told yourself is "Yes, but... I have to break a commitment to myself to be there for you. It's okay. You're more important than I am."

And while you're being a good friend to your friend, you've just started an internal dialogue between a few of your different selves. One self is proud of you for being a good friend. Another self is hurt and angry that you've allowed yourself to be pulled away. Your worst self is likely saying something like, "Ha! Proof you'll never get your book done. Any excuse to avoid the work, right?"

Can you think of a way to turn this into a "Yes, and..." situation, where you can be true to both your friend and yourself?

How about, "Yes, I'm here for you *and* I'll be able to give you my 100% focus in one hour. Can I call you back then?"

You put your phone on airplane mode, set your alarm for one hour so that you're not distracted, worrying about and checking the time to make sure you actually do call her back in an hour. And then you get back to what you were doing for your book. That's a "Yes, and..." answer.

Or how about, "Yes, I'm here for you, but I can only talk now for ten minutes, so let's set up a lunch for tomorrow. (Then get off that phone in ten minutes).

Now, what if the competing distraction is internal—not coming from an outside interrupter but from your own brain? This is what Gloria Mark of the University of

California, Irvine studied and reported on in *The Cost of Interrupted Work: More Speed and Stress*. Looking at productivity in workplaces, tracking the second-by-second activities of 48 research subjects, she found that about half of all interruptions are self-interruptions.

These are interruptions like reacting to that gentle but compelling 'ping' sound your computer makes when you have a new message.

It's certainly easy for me to echo common advice like "turn off your notifications," or "shut down apps like email and texts that alert you to new activity." And really, clicking the "off" button is simple… except that it's clearly not easy since so many writers just can't do it. We find rational-sounding reasons to stay connected to the distractions that trigger self-interruption.

How about some data to help you at least try shutting out those self-interruptions. According to Mark it takes an average of 23 minutes and 15 seconds to get back to the task and the level of focus you had before the interruption.

And the cost to you, aside from it taking much longer to complete your scrappy rough draft?

Mark reported that "after only 20 minutes of interrupted performance people reported significantly higher stress, frustration, workload, effort, and pressure."

So, how can you "Yes, and…" self-interruptions? One way is to set short, clear writing sprints that allow you to take a break every certain number of minutes, like the Pomodoro approach where one focuses for 25 minutes on a task then takes a 5-minute break. Some research posits that our focus and performance start to deteriorate after 50-60 minutes of continuous work and that taking rest breaks every 40 minutes help us maintain or resume our focus more quickly.

So, if you set a timer to work with full focus for between 25 and 40 minutes, your "Yes, and…" to also appease your curiosity about what's new in your inbox or social media feed might be, "I will write with full focus until my alarm tells me it is time to take a quick break and then I will give in to my FOMO (fear of missing out) and check email and social media for ten minutes."

Using this approach I learned how to actually shut down my email program entirely, some days forgetting to turn it on again, much to the chagrin of my husband who relies on me allowing external interruptions to entertain his self-interruptions at work!

Your Turn

Think about all of the interruptions that you contend with when you've committed to time on your book.

- Is it people opening the door to your quiet space and taking you out of the flow?
- Is it kids who track you down and need you to find a lost Lego piece?
- Is it pop-up notifications on your desktop that provide an excuse to "just have a quick peek?"

Write down all of the ways you have, in the past, allowed yourself to be pulled away from your writing time, whether by others or by your own self.

Write down all of the ways you can imagine being pulled off-course when you're in your special writing time.

Now, for each of those distractions, write down a "Yes, and…" response that will allow you, without guilt, to keep your commitment to yourself and respond in a caring way to the person who is distracting you—and yes, this applies even (maybe even especially) when *you* are your own worst distraction.

8

CHOOSING 'THIS AND THAT,' NOT 'THIS OR THAT'

"There's always another option. There's always another one. It's never only 'this' or 'that,' the moon or else the sun. Don't sigh and choose the greater or lesser of two plights. But look to see the stars beyond for options vast and bright." ~Richelle E. Goodrich

On the surface, "this and that" sounds similar to "yes, and…" but the two approaches to grabbing control of your writing time are quite different. While "yes, and…" helps you set boundaries to protect your writing time, "this and that" thinking helps you find ways to bundle activities so your book work is layered with non-negotiable activities.

It may sound glib, but "this *and* that" thinking has entirely changed my approach to virtually all areas of life. And it all started with dessert.

If I had to sum up my brother in one sentence it would be the following,

"Derek is the master of this *and* that. Whenever asked to choose between two options that both sound good, his response is inevitably, *Why choose this* **or** *that, why not this* **and** *that?*"

Derek lived with my family for a time and one way he contributed to our household was by making dinner five nights a week. One night he said, "I feel like making dessert. What would you like?"

I said, "Mom's brownies or your apple crisp."

To which Derek replied, "Why does it have to be brownies or crisp? Why can't it be both?"

Not only did we have the best dessert night *ever*, we also discovered a new way of thinking about the way we deal with competing interests in our house. With our new "this *and* that" approach to decision-making, we now just naturally brainstorm the ways we can all have our cake and eat it, too, since what is the point of uneaten cake? The ideas will often be ridiculous and impossible, but with the belief that everybody can win, we usually find a way to meet everyone's needs and desires.

It was easy to see the relevance of choosing two desserts in my work, as well. As a coach, all of the writers I've worked with have been juggling responsibilities that include a job and/or parenting and/or caring for an aging parent and/or needing to spend some quality time with their spouse. I've yet to meet a writer who does not have time constraints placed on them by their competing roles in life.

So, how can you apply the "this and that" approach to scheduling time in a day that doesn't have extra minutes to spare? The first step is to actually look at all of the things you do in your day and make a list of those activities.

Then, ask the question, "how can I do that thing *and* work on my book?"

This is an exercise in being both super specific and thinking broadly.

Let's say you commute to work for thirty minutes each way. That's an hour of the day that most people say they can't work on their book. Well, certainly, unless you have a self-driving vehicle (Lord help us) you can't be typing words into your manuscript if you're behind the wheel, but if you think more broadly, there are lots of things you could be doing to further progress on your book.

Perhaps you could take transit and type on a laptop or tablet. Now you're commuting *and* writing your book.

What if you need to be in your car? You could use your commute time to listen to inspiring podcasts about writing or writers, or an audio book in your genre to help you improve your craft. Even one idea from a half-hour commute could be a springboard to more words in your own story.

Not a commuter? Maybe you're a parent who is also the chief cook and bottle-washer, chauffeur, cheerleader, and clean underwear ensurer. Oh, and you have a day job, too. How can you incorporate "this *and* that" scheduling to include work on your book when you're already doing this, that *and the other thing* all at the same time?

Could you use dictation software to "write" scenes while you sit at soccer practice or wait in the car to pick up dawdling kids from after school activities?

Specifically, think in small chunks of time, like ten minutes. Can you take a shower *and* run through scenarios that would drive your heroine to put olive oil in a neighbour's shampoo bottle?

Can you use the voice recording function on your phone to dictate story ideas or scenes *and* ignore the funny looks you get from other shoppers as you walk around the grocery store?

Can you visit your aging parent *and* type or handwrite notes while your mom is watching her show, not looking for your conversation, just happy for your company?

Even when you're not able to put words on the page (or into a digital recording device) you can be working on your book. When life is so scheduled you sometimes feel like you're packing two lives into one, it's important to give yourself credit for the non-writing activities that are helping you build your writing skills. It's important to keep a positive mindset about your ability to *one day* have the space to complete your scrappy rough draft.

Your Turn

Over to you. If you've done the Your Turn exercise connected to Chapter 6, **Why you'll never create the time**

to write, you've already got the information you need to find your "this and that" spaces in your day or week.

If you've not yet done it, I suggest you do it before you start this Your Turn exercise.

If you did the Chapter 6 exercise and found that you truly do not have one single 10-minute block of unscheduled time on any day of your week that you can do the thing you need to do *and* work on your book...well, perhaps this is not the right time to be working on your scrappy rough draft.

Many of us have seasons in our lives when we have to accept that the work that is important to us, but not urgent, must be set aside.

That said, not being able to schedule time to do all that you have to do and work on your book is different from *deciding* you don't have time. If you're not sure which situation you're in, skip this exercise for now, keep reading, and come back to "this *and* that" when you're ready.

If you're certain you can't apply "this *and* that" scheduling, put this book down and buy one that has tools to help you find balance in your life. Not joking.

9

WHO ARE YOU? WHO, WHO? WHO, WHO?

"Recurring themes in your writing is a strength. Those issues that matter to you, that keep recurring in your life, that keep you awake, you might see them as weaknesses in your day-to-day life, but in writing they are your personal gold mine. Tap your own emotional resources for what matters to you, because when you write about those things that matter your story resonates with passion and authority and purpose." ~Laura Baker, WriterUniv (email to author, Jan 14, 2019)

Writers often joke—and are the butt of jokes—about having multiple voices in our heads. We have the voices of our characters who speak to us when we're in the flow, telling us what they'd say in certain situations and sometimes, when we're really lucky, commandeering our stories to tell the ones that they want told.

We also have at least one voice that assumes the role of an inner critic. You know the one—the unsolicited advice about what's best for us and why we'd be wise to set aside this silly dream of becoming an author. Even after we've been published and can wear the author label with pride, this voice doesn't leave most authors. It just changes its nag track to how we are not and never will be as good/rich/successful/prolific/beautiful as Nora Roberts.

Those are the voices that virtually every writer shares, no matter how many titles they've had published.

Based on the "multiple self" research, every one of us has many other voices in our inner chatter choirs. Naming and bringing one of those voices to life is what this exercise is focused on.

As I later explain in Chapter 14, **Goal-setting versus domain and direction planning,** we all respond to impositions on our time in different ways, depending on what is needing to get done.

Imagine you're a parent and you have a child who's in a sport that requires they be driven to practice for 6:00 AM on weekdays or that you attend games that last all afternoon, every Saturday from April to October. Do you want to be wearing a chauffeur cap or waving cheerleading pompoms for all these hours a week? Some days, maybe, but probably not *every* day.

But you do it. You make the commitment and you follow through since you are a parent who supports your child's hobbies. It's part of who you are and how you self-define.

If you're not a parent, perhaps you practice a sport or engage in a serious hobby that imposes on your time—not always but sometimes. Your own Saturday morning ice time means you can't stay out drinking with friends on Friday night, so you're the first to head home because your team needs you to be well-slept.

So how does this relate to writing your scrappy rough draft? Good question and an easy answer—from a neuroscience point of view.

For thousands of years, Buddhist Monks have said that there is no constant self, that *nothing* is constant and everything changes through time. And recently, a University of British Columbia professor and researcher, Evan Thompson, confirmed that brain neuroplasticity gives us the ability to evolve and consciously become the kind of person we want to be.

Although this may not sound like news—anyone who does yoga or meditates likely shares that Buddhist belief—what is new is the neuroscientific evidence that, according to Thompson,

> *"from a neuroscience perspective, the brain and body is constantly in flux. There's nothing that corresponds to the sense that there's an unchanging self."*

The good news, if it's not clear, is that your brain is ready and primed, just by the nature of it being your brain, to add a new, productive writer self to your ever-changing list of selves.

Your Turn

This isn't a "sit down and think" exercise, it's a top-of-mind list. There are no wrong answers.

Step 1: Set your timer for two minutes and write as many answers to the following question you can think of.

Who are you?

For example, I wrote:

1. Writer
2. Empath
3. Funny
4. Creative
5. Tall
6. Prematurely grey
7. Wife
8. Mother
9. Writing Coach
10. Compassionate
11. Snarky
12. Woman of a certain age
13. Quebecker
14. Atheist
15. Business partner
16. Professional

17. Perfectionist
18. Dedicated

Step 2: Organize your self-definitions into categories

All of those words that you wrote down in Step 1 are the ways you self-define. And odds are that you've written down self-definitions that fall into a few different categories which we now need to disentangle.

First rewrite all of the words that would be considered your social roles — words like mother, sister, daughter, woodworker, cashier, volunteer, etc.—across the top of your page.

Mine are: *Writer, wife, mother, business partner, writing coach.*

Next, circle all of the words that would be considered personality or character traits and then add those words below your social roles as appropriate. For instance, "caring" would be a trait that you could include with mother/sister/daughter and with volunteer. "Attentive to details" could fit with woodworker and cashier.

Mine are: *Dedicated, perfectionist, professional, snarky, compassionate, creative, funny*

What words remain? You may have some that refer to your physical traits—auburn, tall, hard-of-hearing. If you can see a direct way your physical traits relate to your social role, add them below the roles with the personality traits, otherwise you can ignore them.

Mine are: *Tall, prematurely grey*

And finally, if you have words that fall into what psychologists call "existential statements"—I am a human being, I am a child of the universe—treat them the way you did the physical traits. If they make sense to include below one of your social roles, add them. If not, ignore them.

Mine are: *woman of a certain age, atheist, Quebecker, empath.*

The top-level words, your social roles, can also be classified as your self-aspects. These self-aspects shape the way we think of ourselves and how we manage our day-to-day lives. So, the question now is, Did you identify either "writer" or "author" as a self-aspect?

If not, this is kind of good news since it means that you have a somewhat easy answer to why it's been hard to make a commitment to your words.

If you did identify "writer" or "author" but only since we've been talking about your writer self for the last 35 pages, well done. The Jedi mind tricks are working.

If "writer" or "author" is a way that you've self-identified for a while now, congratulations! You've got perhaps the most critical foundational block already in place.

Step 3: Identify your writer's attributes

The next step is to identify the attributes that you associate with being a writer or author.

The benefit of naming your writer attributes is when the *shoulds* of being a writer are drowned out by the *wants* of one of your other aspects. You have some clear expectations of your writer self that are equal in importance to your other aspects.

In one group I asked the writers to name the attributes of their writer/author aspects and they came up with a wide range of words, from "mercenary" to "advocate." These simple words are actually quite rich in meaning since they tell some deep stories about why these writers sit down to write, if not every day, often enough to call themselves writers and authors.

For instance, the author who named her primary attribute as "mercenary" explained that she writes to support herself; writing novels and non-fiction books is her primary source of income. That drives her writing in a direction that is quite different from the writer who said her primary attribute is "advocate."

Another author who has two novels published with small publishers used the word "frustrated," which was stated as a bit of a joke. However, there is often truth in jokes, especially the ones we make about ourselves. When we dug deeper into the meaning behind the attribute, he explained that his books are not generating enough income to even support the costs of hiring an editor and entering writing contests.

So, the million-dollar question is whether he could achieve his financial goals if he articulated one of his writer's attributes as something that connects to his desire to earn a living with his fiction. And from a goal-setting perspective, it would be helpful to also articulate if "earn a living" meant $1,000 a month, a week, or a day. The approach to reaching these different goals would be quite different. Not just from a marketing perspective, but also the genre of the books he chooses to write to how many of them he publishes each a year.

And that will also impact the attributes he chooses to describe himself as an author.

If you have one story in you that's been trying to be told for years, your starting place may be simply to get that one story told and then go from there.

In that case your attributes may include traits like, "passionate," "focused," and "honouring."

If, on the other hand, you're a writer who has a dozen stories all clumped up inside you vying for your attention, and you find this competition for your storytelling overwhelming, you might choose words like, "creative," "focused," and "finisher," as your primary writer's attributes.

And that's the next step of this exercise. To take some time to think of the words that resonate with how you see yourself—or would like to see yourself—as a writer or author.

You may find these words already on your list, or you may want to add new words.

One final time, using my own exercise as an example, I could create the following diagram that shows my self-concept which includes my multiple self-aspects (top row) and associated attributes (left column):

Writer: dedicated, perfectionist, snarky, funny, creative

Business partner: professional, creative

Writing coach: professional, compassionate

Wife: Snarky, compassionate, funny

Mother: Compassionate, dedicated

DONNA

	Writer	Biz Partner	Coach	Wife	Mother
Snarky	●			●	
Perfectionist	●				
Dedicated	●				●
Creative	●	●			
Professional		●	●		
Compassionate			●	●	●
Loving				●	●
Funny	●			●	

10

THE SCIENCE OF THE INNER CRITIC

*"I want to write what I do not know, in ways I have not written.
I need to speed ahead of the censor and write so fast my velocity
causes the accidents of insight and language that make good
writing." ~Donald Murray*

One thing I struggled to understand about my process when I decided to write a novel was why I found sitting down to work on a creative story so hard when I could write non-fiction for clients quickly, easily, and well. I mean, it's all just words, right? At the time I was writing those first words of that first manuscript, I'd been paid to be a go-to word person for fifteen years. I had confidence and an ego that had no problem being told when I got something wrong and had to write it again.

Okay, I'd think, *Let's try it this way, then.* And I would. In most cases, if I missed the mark on try #1, it hit the Bull's

Eye on try #2. When I write for clients, I don't need to write a scrappy rough draft. I can simply write.

And so, I approached my first manuscript with a confidence that I quickly and painfully realized was entirely undeserved.

And this led me to ask, "Why?" and then to go searching for an answer. I read lots about the Inner Critic, who, it surprised me to learn, had joined me on my writing process.

I'm guessing you're familiar with the concept of inner critics and negative self-talk. Many writers work with coaches to help them identify who that voice really belongs to—a Grade 4 English teacher who humiliated you when you read your "About My Family" short story in front of the class, or a relative who only ever found fault with your creative writing, or any one of a thousand different people and experiences.

Some coaches suggest we kick that negative ninny out with no apology.

A cautionary tale

If you're someone who has wished to be rid of every iota of inner critic once and for all, I say, *Be careful what you wish for.*

There is a psychological condition called hypergraphia which is the result of an abnormal interaction between the frontal and temporal lobes of the brain. It's so abnormal, in fact, the temporal lobe acts as though it doesn't even exist.

For people who experience hypergraphia it's as if their inner critic has been murdered.

And when a writer's frontal lobe activity takes over, leaving the temporal lobe entirely inactive, the compulsion to write is so great that people who have this behavioural condition cannot *not* write.

Does this mean that the tsunami of words will be publishable? Not at all. They'll still be scrappy rough draft words, but there will be an endless supply of them.

Some people who have this condition use it to their benefit. It's believed that many prolific authors have (or had) hypergraphia including Lewis Carroll, Isaac Asimov, Danielle Steele, Joyce Carol Oates, and a couple of authors who are held as the gold standard of how we should write every day for at least four hours—Stephen King and Nora Roberts (who actually writes for eight hours a day).

Loving your Inner Critic

Back to managing that voice we writers have to listen to inside our heads: my challenge was that no matter how hard I tried, I could never pinpoint that person or experience that was taking up space in my brain. I was lucky enough to only consciously remember being encouraged in most things I tried my hand at, whether it was something I was naturally talented with at something I had to work hard to figure out.

And then I met Cami Ostman, an author and writer coach with twenty years of experience as a therapist. Cami draws on the family systems theory in her counselling. Her approach to handling our Inner Critic was something I'd not seen before. It resonated.

Cami argues that our Inner Critic is not trying to ruin our lives with its warnings and efforts to keep us from writing. She maintains that voice was given a role at some point in our life to protect us from something—probably not at all related to writing. Its intentions are good, but its advice is misdirected. She argues that it's counter-productive to vilify the voice since the voice is part of us and it's never helpful to bad talk your own brain.

What felt right about that approach was the focus on self-compassion. I still wasn't able to find the source of my insecurities related to creative writing, but it no longer mattered. I was able to hear those cautionary words and let them go since I knew that my resistance was coming from a source that was trying to be helpful and was not related to the words I was trying to move from my brain to the page.

But, since I'm a perpetual three-year-old, constantly asking "Why?" I needed more information about how this subconscious process works. That led me to the research of Joseph Ledoux, PhD, and his findings about how our brains react to situations that cause fear—even irrational situations like frantically jumping away from a ball of fluff on the floor that, for an instant, we perceive to be a spider. Or, extrapolating, finding a hundred-and-one reasons why we can't sit down to write.

It's not a stretch since the brain process is the same whether we're avoiding perceived (or real) *physical* danger or perceived (or real) *emotional* danger. It all comes down to the relationship between two parts of our brain: the cortex and the amygdala.

Chapter 20, **Skulking around the writer's block** goes into detail about this relationship between the two, but the relevance here is that your inner critic is taking its lead from your cautious amygdala.

When your amygdala is active in your writing process, it has taken over the driver's seat, but is clever enough to convince you that it's simply a cautious back-seat driver. So we, the rational writer, try to explain why we're resistant to scheduling and sticking to a time to work on our books. We come up with reasons that the critic nods its head at and supports—

If I was meant to write this book it would have been written by now, you think. Your inner critic agrees.

I'm not smart enough to accomplish what less than one in ten thousand people can pull off, you rationalize. Your inner critic nods its amygdalian head.

And with the confirmation that this goal is fool-hardy, you make yourself feel better by making it impossible to adjust your schedule to include time to write and you say things like, "Maybe I'll have time once the kids have moved away and I've retired."

Unfortunately, even when external influencers are as perfect as they can be, your internal influencers—that pesky limbic system of your brain that takes over when it perceives a threat—will still be with you.

So, to break that pattern of procrastination, you need to approach your desk, laptop, or notebook, a little differently; you need to approach your words with a new understanding of what's happening behind-the-scenes. The good news is that you don't have to understand *why* this is, you "simply" have to identify *how* you react when your rational cortex has been dethroned by your "act, don't think" amygdala, so that you can reseat your cortex in its rightful place.

We tend to think of the word procrastination with judgement: *It's a bad thing to do.* And yet, we all do it. Writers are exceptionally good at procrastination. I can't tell you how many of my friends say that their homes are never cleaner than when they have a writing deadline.

The problem with procrastination is not really that we're not writing when we scheduled that time to work on our books, it's the fact that we beat ourselves up for it. We hand the mic to our inner critic and give it the stage. And once it's done its monologue, the rational and creative parts of our brain have basically shut down, unable to function with all the emotion and noise.

We need to pre-empt that situation and one way to do that is to recognize that we need to ease into our writing habit and redefine what that can look like.

Productive procrastination

It used to be that as soon as I decided it was time to write, I'd have a burning desire to tidy up the kitchen (which, in a house with three other people, is always in need of tidying). It was a good, productive procrastination exercise since I'd approach the dishes and counters and compost bin with thoughts about my work-in-progress.

But after many months of being the kitchen elf, I started to resent that activity, so rather than being able to mindlessly clean and consciously ponder my book, I'd fret and fume about why a grown-ass man was incapable of rinsing the coffee pot when he took the last cup, and what kind of therapy might help a teenager understand that placing his dirty bowl on the counter *above* the dishwasher was like leaving me to flush away his morning constitution — something he'd thankfully stopped doing when he was four years old.

I needed to find other ways to productively procrastinate for ten minutes while my brain warmed up to the idea that it would be working soon. I recognized that when I wasn't in a rush to shower and get out the door, showering was a creative time for me. I'd not have to be actively thinking about my work-in-progress, but the act of washing my hair often triggered something worth exploring once I sat down to write. So, I connected my productive procrastination to personal hygiene and let the kitchen remain in chaos until after I was done my words.

But then, in one of my mastermind groups, three of the five participants mentioned that they did Morning Pages *every day*. I'd tried the approach of writing three pages, by hand, each morning before doing anything else (including checking email) which Julia Cameron suggests in her book *The Artist's Way,* many times over the last twenty years. I never managed a week. But something changed when I tried again in 2018. It stuck.

Part of what I did differently was to overlay the Morning Pages free-writing with the Pomodoro Approach—setting a timer for 25 minutes of focused time, followed by a five-minute rest. So instead of writing three pages, I wrote for 25 minutes. I knew that I responded well to having time pressure and constraints so that was my parameter. On most days I wrote five or six pages in my journal. And then, as soon as I finished those pages, I stood up, refreshed my coffee then slid right into working on my manuscript for another half-hour. And it worked like a charm.

That is productive procrastination. For me.

For you, it may be spending fifteen minutes knitting. Or playing an instrument. Or colouring. Or going for a walk.

The goal is to give your brain something to do that it's not afraid of, something that doesn't trigger your fight, flight or freeze reaction. When you're in this mental and emotional safe space you can be thinking about your manuscript without triggering the fear factor.

Flexible productivity

Like a fraternal twin to productive procrastination, flexible productivity is another way to embrace the time you're not writing as time you still acknowledge and value as working on your book.

The reality is that I can easily type 1200 words in an hour. When I'm really focused and know exactly where I'm going, I can double that word count. So, if I were to set the goal of writing a 50,000 word book, it *should* take me about 42 hours to write that scrappy rough draft. Again, by extension, I *should* be able to get that done in a week, assuming I don't have client work.

But how long did the scrappy rough draft of this book (which was 50,000 words) take to write? I estimate that it took me more than double those 42 hours of fingers tapping keys to get my first draft done since not all minutes are focused minutes. And, for every hour I spent typing what you're reading (well, a highly edited version of what I originally wrote), I spent at least six hours thinking, reading and researching.

In addition, I was working as a coach, doing at least ten hours of admin work every week in the Creative Academy, writing and publishing a blog post each day on Medium, co-authoring a novella, and doing ghost writing for my technical writing clients. So, a book that one might think *should* have only taken me a week to write? It actually took me over four months just to complete the scrappy rough draft.

Did I ever beat myself up about how long it was taking? No. Okay… yes, a little. Did I ever have days where I knew I could have done better, been more focused? Sure. But the fact is that I showed up, maybe not every day, but enough times to get this book done.

Since I'm a trained professional (meaning my bum is trained to be sat upon for 8-hours-a-day), one hour of straight writing is physically easy for me. Also, since writing has been my job for over twenty years, my writing area of my brain is well-developed.

But if you're not used to sitting for long periods of time or typing ideas is new to you, fifteen minutes might be a more appropriate goal as you build your writing habit. Think of your writing muscle the same way you'd think of other muscles.

If you were to ask me to go jogging for an hour in my current state of physical fitness, I wouldn't even bother putting on my sneakers. But if you said I only had to do a jog/walk combination for five minutes, alternating between the two speeds, I could wrap my head around that. And then after a few days of five minutes, adding a minute would be possible. Then a minute more. Soon, if I was crazy enough to think running was a good idea, I'd be joining my sister in half marathons. (Lucky for both of us, we have a non-compete clause in our relationship so I will never feel guilty about not training my body to move faster than a saunter.)

Your Turn

Exercise 1: Productive procrastination

Here's one approach to help you reprogram that feeling you may have of facing a blank page, of the resistance that either keeps you from even sitting down to work on your scrappy rough draft, or, once you are seated, gives you a hundred-and-one other things that you need to do before you start to write.

You'll need to set aside between 45 and 60 minutes to do this full exercise and you may need to do it several times to see the change. Think of it like a medicine that needs to build up in your body before you feel the full effect of it.

But once you've gained control of your cortex and have a quick way to push past your resistance to give your inner critic somewhere else to focus, you'll be able to eliminate this exercise.

Make a list of all the possible ways you could safely ease into your next scheduled writing session.

The next time your timer goes off to let you know it's time to work on your manuscript, start by doing one of the safe activities on your list. See how that impacts the way you feel once you sit down at your desk.

Something may work for a while and then stop working. And you'll know when it stops working (or doesn't work to start with) since you'll either not be casually thinking about your characters or the research you'd like to do when you sit down to work, or, when you do sit down, you'll still be faced by inner chatter that keeps you from approaching your book with confidence and joy.

Exercise 2: Flexible productivity

Set your timer for three minutes and free write the answer to the four questions that follow. Write until the timer goes off. Don't stop writing even if you're writing gibberish.

Step 1

For the first question, be so specific you feel silly. Include things as apparently inane as the colour of the leggings you'll be wearing (nobody still wears pants when they write, do they?), the essential oil you'll have in your diffuser, and the flavour of tea/coffee/juice/wine/whisky you'll have in your mug or glass.

Here's your first question:

If I could wake up tomorrow morning with my writer habit already a regular part of my routine, what would that habit look like on a daily or weekly basis?

Step 2

Your next challenge is to free write for three minutes about what your future could look like as the author of your book. The trick here is not to write a list of lots of things, but to go deep on one imagined future state.

For instance, if you answer that finishing your book will give you credibility, take that deeper. What do you expect increased credibility to provide you with? Is it more clients in your business? Is it new respect from your family? Is it something internal, like more confidence? Whatever that answer is, go deeper. Keep going deeper until the timer goes off. If you had other ideas pop up, repeat the process.

Here's the second question:

What opportunities, for you and/or for your readers, will open up once you're sharing your story or book?

Step 3

The next three-minute, free-writing exercise invites you to be ridiculous. Don't worry that you'll be held to these ideas. For instance, a few years ago I wrote that I'd be willing to give up my first-born to achieve my writing goals... that I'd be willing to give up cooking meals for the family (that one is 100% true)... that I'd be willing to give up an hour of sleep in the morning... haha! (*Never!*)

Here's the question:

What are you willing to give up to finish writing your scrappy rough draft?

Step 4

The final three-minutes is to think about all the different ways you can connect to your work-in-progress in small, 5- to 10-minute increments, that you could schedule into the small windows of time you have throughout the day.

Here's the final question:

What specific things can I do in service of completing my book when I only have five to ten minutes to work on it?

11

HARNESSING THE POWER OF "YES...
BUT..."

*"We are products of our past, but we don't have to be prisoners
of it." ~Rick Warren*

While using the power of "Yes, and..." thinking can help you manage your time to protect space for working on your scrappy rough draft, sometimes you'll sit down and be faced with an inner critic who thinks you could or should be using your time differently, perhaps in its words, more wisely. In that situation, you might benefit from a nice, strong use of the word, "but."

Here's how that works. Imagine happily working on your manuscript and despite having done the prep to quiet your inner critic, it's awake and starts to chat. It interrupts your flow, whispering sweet nothings in your head like:

"Your draft is terrible."

"You are such a slow writer."

"You're older than most successful authors, you know."

Rather than trying to convince yourself otherwise since there will be some amount of truth, at least in your mind, about the statement, use the power of "but" to change the future. You reply to that negative inner voice or thought with one like this:

"*Yes*, my draft is terrible right now, *but* once I finish it, I can start the editing process. This is exactly how authors get their books written, in stages starting with a scrappy rough draft."

"*Yes*, I am a slow writer, *but* if I write just 500 words a day I'll have my draft done in about six months. That's an entirely reasonable goal.

"*Yes*, I am older than many successful authors, *but* I have so much more life experience than those young whipper snappers that I can inject into my stories to make them richer. My age is a benefit to my craft."

It can be easier to quiet that negative inner voice by agreeing with it and giving it more information to chew on, so being prepared with a logical response to your inner critic's common concerns might help you to get back to the important work you're doing, quickly and with less angst.

That said, some mindset and happiness coaches argue that there is no point in arguing with our inner critic since, for every reason you can come up with for why you need not listen to it, it will come up with another.

Personally, when I add the "but" and a future vision of myself and my work potential, I can almost always quiet my inner critic. But I've had decades of experience doing this!

If you're newer to the approach, perhaps adding another step, a variation on Byron Katie's method to question and change thoughts and beliefs, might help.

In Katie's book, *Loving What Is: The Four Questions That Can Change Your Life,* she suggests we can change thought patterns by asking the following questions:

- Is it true?
- Can you absolutely know that it's true?
- How do you react, what happens, when you believe that thought?
- Who would you be without the thought?

In our situation, as a writer working on a scrappy rough draft of a book, sometimes a gentle adjustment to the second question can be more powerful since in our situation we might actually be able to answer, "Yes, it is absolutely true that I am a slow writer," and that wouldn't help quiet the unhelpful inner critic.

In those situations we can change the second question to,

- Will this *always* be true?

Odds are that you will be able to imagine a future when you can write more quickly or change whatever situation your critic is warning you about. If you can answer, "No" to "will this always be true?" then you have an argument that you can frame as a "yes...but..."

Here are several nasty whispers I collected from the inner critics of Creative Academy members. I've asked the questions, "Is it true?" and "Can you absolutely know that it's true" or "Will this always be true?" and categorized each one as either a possible truth or a lie.

- You have no right to write about things you have not experienced yourself. (lie)
- Your story is trivial. (possible truth)
- Writing is too hard. (lie)
- Why bother? It'll never be finished. (lie)
- What if my story is terrible and never gets published? (possible truth)
- What if my story gets published and everyone hates it? (lie)
- You're not creative enough. (lie)
- Everything you've written is cliche. (lie)
- You can't write *this* scene until you figure out something else. (possible truth)
- My words don't matter. (lie)
- You know nothing, Jon Snow. (hilarious)
- I'm not good enough. (possible truth)
- I'm a shitty writer. (possible truth)
- I'm bored. I should watch TV instead. (possible truth)
- I don't have anything to say. (possible truth)
- I have nothing to say. (lie)
- I don't have any more good stories left. I had a good run but now I am done. (lie)
- Even if your book is any good, there are so many books out there already, nobody will ever find it and buy it. (lie)

- This book will never sell. (lie)
- This book will be a failure. (lie)
- My prose could be stronger. (possible truth)
- My vocabulary should be richer. (possible truth)
- My flow of sentences is not good enough. (possible truth)

Some lies are easy to identify. If a statement is written with an absolute like "never," "always," "everything," or "nothing" it is an automatic lie. Others are a bit more challenging but if it's clear that time or experience can change the statement, it's a lie.

For instance, "writing is *too* hard," is a lie since it may be hard today but could be easy tomorrow or next week or after you figure out why your protagonist decided to change her career mid-story.

"Writing is hard," however, is a possible truth. Some days writing is hard. Some scenes are hard to write. Some characters hide their motivation from you. This challenge can be written with a positive outcome though. For instance,

> Yes, writing is hard, but the reward of finishing my story will be worth the work. Or,

> Yes, writing is hard sometimes, but some days it flows so easily I forget to eat.

Sometimes we need to take our negative voice and rewrite it so that it's both truthful and focuses on the future potential, whether it's a lie or a possible truth. For example, if we take a common inner critic lie, "My words don't matter," this could be reimagined as,

> Sure, right now my words might only matter to me, but once I finish my story they could impact one person or one million people...I won't know until the book is finished and shared.

Your reply to "This book will be a failure" could be,

> My book might not achieve the goals I have for it, but the only real failure is quitting before I give myself and my book a chance to try to succeed.

Give it a try with your own negative beliefs about your writing in the Your Turn exercises that follow.

Your Turn

If you have negative beliefs about the quality or quantity of your scrappy rough draft or your process to get it written, approach this exercise with the intention of having fun. You're playing with words, after all!

Step 1

Write down as many of the awful things your inner critic tells you as you can handle.

Step 2

Break the criticisms into two groups: those that are *actually* true and those that can be proven to *not* be true.

Step 3

Take the list of negative beliefs that are true and finish it with an affirming statement. So you'd write, "Yes, <your negative thought>, but <your positive belief or fact>."

And example could be, "My vocabulary should be richer but this is just my first draft and right now what matters is getting the story down. Enriching the vocabulary is a job for the editing stage."

Step 4

For the beliefs that can be proven to be lies—or gross exaggerations—revise them to be truthful statements. The truth may not be the opposite, but it will likely have some potential to be positive.

For instance, "This book will never sell" is easy to identify as a lie since you cannot predict the future of a still-to-be-written book. A more truthful statement would be, "This book has the potential to sell lots of copies." Now add the positive ending, "but until it's written and edited, it won't sell any—so I better get back to the work of finishing my scrappy rough draft!"

12

HARNESSING THE POWER OF "...YET"

"I don't divide the world into the weak and the strong, or the successes and the failures...I divide the world into the learners and the non-learners." ~Benjamin Barber

What if the voices in your head are saying things that don't fit the "yes...but..." approach to reminding yourself that your scrappy rough draft is not only *allowed* to have flaws and holes and tense challenges, it's *supposed* to have things to fix in the revisions stage?

This may not feel like the most natural belief since we live in a world that celebrates—and exaggerates—so-called natural talent. It suggests that some people are born to be great at certain things while the rest of us have no hope of achieving great things. Of course, this isn't true. But the message is repeated so often it's hard not to believe it.

If you struggle with beliefs about your writing or writing process that tell you you're just not good enough, that you've failed before so you'll likely fail again, perhaps the work done by Stanford University psychologist Dr. Carol Dweck on the growth mindset is what will help you face your manuscript with the confidence you need.

The basic premise of the growth mindset is that people who believe they can learn new skills get smarter. Their brains continue to grow and behave differently when faced with failure. These people take on challenges knowing that they can increase their abilities and improve their results. And research shows that people with a growth mindset achieve higher levels of success than those who have a fixed mindset.

People with a fixed mindset believe intelligence is static. They typically avoid challenges, give up easily, ignore useful negative feedback and feel threatened by the success of others. People with a fixed mindset do not believe intelligence can be developed. These folks do not like challenges, give up in the face of obstacles, respond poorly to criticism, and can be envious of other people's success.

If you're like me, you can see yourself exhibiting traits at both ends of the fixed-growth mindset continuum, depending on the situation—or day. We're what Dr. Dweck classifies as having a mixed mindset.

If you already have a growth mindset, or are in a good mixed mindset headspace, taking your inner critic's caution and adding the word "yet" to the end of it may be enough to help you maintain your writing momentum when you start to worry that your work isn't good enough.

"Yet" communicates that you're on a learning curve and gives you a path into the future.

If you hear that voice tell you anything that starts with "You can't..." change it to the first person and add, "yet" to the thought.

"You can't make the conflict in this scene compelling enough," becomes, "I can't make the conflict in this scene compelling enough, *yet*."

"You don't know how to publish a book" becomes, "I don't know how to publish a book, *yet*."

Drawing on the power of a growth mindset, you'll find the resources to help you learn the skills you need to edit that scene into a compelling one when you get to the revision stage (which is *not* while you're working on your scrappy rough draft, anyway) and either submit your manuscript to agents or publishers or learn the stages of indie publishing.

Most of our concerns about becoming a published author can be soothed by adopting the growth mindset, by adding that magic, three-letter word "yet" to the fear-based thought.

Your Turn

Do you know if you have a fixed mindset or a growth mindset, as relates to writing your book? One way Dr.

Dweck suggests figuring this out is by doing a simple scan of how you feel when you reach the hard parts of writing (or any activity that you enjoy doing, until it gets hard). If hitting the hard part makes you feel tired, dizzy, bored, or hungry (her list) that is the reaction of a fixed mindset. When this happens, she suggests you choose to put yourself into the growth mindset by "picturing your brain forming new neuron connections as you meet the challenge and learn."

In her book, *Mindset: The New Psychology of Success*, Dr. Dweck wrote,

> *"Mindset change is not about picking up a few pointers here and there. It's about seeing things in a new way. When people...change to a growth mindset, they change from a judge-and-be-judged framework to a learn-and-help-learn framework. Their commitment is to growth, and growth takes plenty of time, effort, and mutual support."*

Thinking about the time, effort and mutual support you've put into or given your scrappy rough draft, what could you be adding more of?

For instance, do you have time to join a mastermind group where you both give and receive support from writer peers? (Creative Academy members meet at least once-a-week in a mastermind setting and many credit the group for helping push through blocks and achieve writing goals more quickly and with less angst).

Do you have a writing friend who would act as an accountability partner for you, and you for them? As simple as it sounds, committing to a supportive friend that you will sit down and write at certain times makes that commitment easier to keep.

What learn-and-help-learn plan can you adopt to help you develop a growth mindset related to your writing and finishing your scrappy rough draft?

If you'd like to see Dr. Dweck's analysis of your mindset, take the mindset assessment on her site, MindsetOnline.com. I did the 16 question quiz and determined that (on a good day) I have one fixed mindset belief and seven growth mindset beliefs. The results told me that the way to apply my mindset most effectively was to buy Dr. Dweck's book (clever!)—but she also shared her four broad steps to change from a fixed to growth mindset:

Step 1: Learn to hear your fixed mindset "voice"

Step 2: Recognize that you have a choice

Step 3. Talk back to it with a growth mindset voice

Step 4: Take the growth mindset action

13

SHOW PASSION THE DOOR AND GET TO KNOW YOUR PURPOSE AS A WRITER

"There are those . . . who think that the man who works with his imagination should allow himself to wait till inspiration moves him. When I have heard such doctrine preached, I have hardly been able to repress my scorn. To me it would not be more absurd if the shoe-maker were to wait for inspiration, or the tallow-chandler for the divine moment of melting. . . . I was once told that the surest aid to the writing of a book was a piece of cobbler's wax on my chair. I certainly believe in the cobbler's wax much more than the inspiration." ~Anthony Trollope

How many times have you read a self-help guru imploring you to "Follow your passion," which brings to mind the scene in *Harry Potter and the Chamber of Secrets* when Ron Weasley says, "Follow the spiders. Why is it always, 'Follow the spiders?' Why can't it ever be, 'Follow the butterflies?'"

I know that years ago, when I was coaching my son on what program to apply to in university, my own conversations with him usually included, "What do you love doing and where is there an overlap with the courses you can take?" Since he loves math and science and is good at them, and since he hates writing and *thinks* he's bad at it, it made sense to take courses that would lead to a Bachelor of Science degree.

Never once did we discuss what he felt his purpose in life was. It may be hard to imagine knowing that when you're only 17 or 18, but it's not impossible. Most of my friends, who are now in their forties to sixties, look back at their childhoods and easily see what their purpose has always been.

My original career goals were to either pursue law enforcement or something within the church. One connection between these two quite different career directions is that they are both helping professions that require an amount of understanding of human psychology. Of course, I didn't know that at the time. But looking back over my life and all the jobs I've had, it's clear that I've always had "be helpful" as my purpose.

And my passion? That's changed many times over the course of my life. In my teens, I could not tell you what I loved doing. But in my twenties, I was passionate about human rights. In my thirties, environmental issues. In my forties giving voice to people who were disenfranchised. I applied my purpose of "being helpful" to working in not-for-profit organizations that campaigned around those issues.

Unlike the advocates and champions I worked alongside, individuals who were clear that their purposes were to save the rainforest or provide safe places for LGBTQ+ teens to be themselves, I could never pick one issue to call my own. I will never be a champion of a single cause since my purpose is too broad. That broad purpose, I believe, is also what gives me the focus to spend hours every day working on creative non-fiction writing, my current passion.

> The difference between passion and purpose is sometimes confusing since they can be the same for some people. But passion is a feeling, it has an inward impact. Purpose is a drive that has an outward impact.

If you've been struggling with a scrappy rough draft that fights you at every paragraph, what researchers have determined about this passion-purpose relationship could help you understand where your challenge lies—and give you a hint about how to address it.

Dr. Morten Hansen is a management professor who was interested in understanding what made bosses judge certain employees as high performers. In his book, *Great at Work: How Top Performers Work Less and Achieve More* he describes a study in which he asked bosses to rank their workers on a performance scale.

Then, Hansen interviewed the employees and asked them to rank themselves on a different scale, one that indicated how much passion they had for their job and how much purpose they felt doing the work.

Not surprisingly, the employees who ranked both their feeling of purpose *and* passion for their job as 'low' were also ranked by their bosses, on average, in the lowest ten percent of performance.

But who would you guess had better performance, the high passion or the high purpose employees? Here's what the research found.

Boss's rank	10/100	20/100	64/100	80/100
Employee's Rank	Low passion/ Low purpose	High passion/ Low purpose	Low passion/ High purpose	High passion/ High purpose

It's clear that knowing and working toward a purpose is more powerful—and makes you do a better job—than having lots of passion.

One of the conclusions Hansen and his research team drew was that having a strong sense of purpose leads to having strong inner motivation. And when you're writing a book, be it your first scrappy rough draft or your tenth revision, inner motivation to get your butt in the chair is critical.

So, thinking about your work-in-progress where are you on the purpose-passion spectrum?

> *"Purpose is your motivation, your why. It brings in action so it focuses on verbs. Purpose completes you."* ~Entrepreneur George Krueger

Figuring out your 'Why?' is an exercise I've seen used in dozens of contexts and one I adapted to use in my course, *Book On Fire*. The original idea comes from Sakichi Toyoda, founder of the Toyota car company. He developed the technique in the 1930s to figure out solutions to production line problems.

In a problem-solution context, the process works by asking the question, 'Why?' to find out the top-of-mind, obvious reason something isn't working its best and then diving deeper to find the real source of the problem by asking 'Why' of each answer.

For example: We missed a shipment deadline. Why? Because the conveyor belt broke. Why? Because it hadn't been serviced in three weeks. Why? Because we're working around the clock due to high sales. Etcetera.

If you're not sure of your writing purpose, your own 'Why' as a writer, the process works just as well.

You have to figure out what your own first 'Why' question is, but here's an example of how the process works in action:

Why am I still thinking about this book idea from ten years ago?

- Because my idea for my main character is one that I've not seen written about.

Why do you want to see a character like the one you're imagining written about?

- Because I believe that a teenager with albinism could be a strong metaphor for all teens who feel different and not understood.

Why is it important for you to tell the story of a teen who doesn't feel she fits in?

- Because one of the leading causes of self-harm and drug and alcohol abuse with teens starts with not feeling valued.

Why does helping teens know that they are valued matter to you?

- Because in raising my own kids I've seen too many teens suffer.

Can you see and feel how different your motivation to finish your book will be once you focus on the reason you're writing that story, as opposed to the fact that you love to write and feel like it's something you could or should do?

If you're wondering how you'll know when you've found your purpose, if you've asked the Why questions enough times, the simple answer is that as soon as you find the person or people your writing will benefit, that's usually where your purpose lies.

- **It may be yourself**—I need to process this story to release and heal from the experiences.
- **It may be a relative**—I need to honour their story so that their contributions aren't forgotten.
- **It may be to strangers**—I need new mothers to recognize the signs of postpartum depression in a novel since they aren't looking for self-help books.

Your Turn

Exercise 1: What is your 'Why'?

Take a deep breath and ask yourself, "Why am I writing this book?" Or perhaps, "Why is this book idea still haunting me after ten years?"

Write the answer, whatever comes to mind.

Now, from that answer, ask your next "Why?"

And so on until you feel like you've hit the kernel of truth, the purpose that you have in writing your book.

Exercise 2: How did your book impact a reader?

Stephen Covey said, "Begin with the end in mind."

If you feel like you need to (or would like to) better understand your purpose in writing your story, take the What is your "Why?" exercise one step further and write a short story about a person who's read your published book and the impact it had on them.

Your book could be fiction or non-fiction, it doesn't matter. Your short story isn't about the book. It's about the person who's benefited from reading it. It will be most powerful if you write from your reader's point of view.

You could wrap this exercise up with a motivational statement such as:

> The purpose of my being a writer is to _____
> for _____.

For example, I wrote,

> The purpose of my being a writer is to <u>create entertaining, creative non-fiction</u> for <u>women who are interested in exploring the impact of culture and religion on their sexuality.</u>

14

GOAL-SETTING VERSUS DOMAIN AND DIRECTIONAL PLANNING

Although a goal is generally assumed to be an end-state,
underlying a goal is often a desire for a longer-term process
rather than a desire for an end-state itself. ~Michael McCaskey,
Harvard Business School

Sometimes, even once we've figured out our writer's self-identity and are clear on our purpose for writing, we still have days when it's easier to read someone else's book than work on our own draft. After I'd published my novel this was where I found myself on more days than not. When I sat my butt in my chair and wasn't able to focus on my scrappy rough draft, I put my attention toward researching why this was happening to me.

The answer to that question came from an area of study that has roots in workplace management.

One challenge managers face is getting workers to do what the company needs them to do when employees have other things that they'd rather be doing. It's framed as a should-versus-want situation, which is similar to the need-versus-want curriculum I used to teach to low-income earners who wanted to learn how to save money.

Here's the challenge for writers:

You know that to get your manuscript finished you should be working on it with an amount of regularity. You know that you need to commit to writing, if not every day, at least to getting a certain number of words written every week. But for some reason, you haven't been hitting that target. Lots of research has been done to show that the slope is slippery once we step away from a project.

Here are some ideas that I believe can add crampons to your soles and keep you from falling down that hill to the place where it feels too hard to get back up again.

The first thing to consider is how you've been thinking about your goal. What language have you been using? People who've worked in certain business settings will be familiar with the SMART goal approach. SMART is an acronym to help us remember to set goals that are Specific, Measurable, Achievable, Realistic and Time-delineated.

If you've followed some variation of the SMART goal approach, you've likely written an end-state goal with a deadline. For instance:

I will finish the 60,000 words for my scrappy rough draft (end-state) by April 1 (deadline).

The challenge for many writers is that you've just applied a logical and analytical frame around a process that is new to you. The actual steps that you'll need to take to get to that end-state are likely ill-defined since you don't yet have the experience to know how many words you can write in a typical day or week.

Not only that, you're applying a left-brain target to a task that will be undertaken by right brain creativity. And, according to researchers, this pits two of our 'selves' against each other and is fertile ground to grow an internal dialogue about what we *should* do and what we *want* to do.

To be clear, this may not be a negative inner critic telling you that you're not up to the task (though it may also have a voice in the conversation). This can be an even harder conversation to control since neither of the voices is being mean or negative, they're simply stating their desires, which are your own totally legitimate, but conflicting desires.

You know you *should* work on your manuscript for at least thirty minutes a day if you're going to get it done by the date you've set as your goal. But you also know that you *want* to have coffee with your best friend (during the time you'd planned to write) or you *want* to read a book in your genre tonight before bed... which means you won't have time to write your own words.

Are you wrong for wanting to connect with an important person in your life or wanting to improve your craft by immersing yourself in fiction? Of course not. It's not wrong, but it can be counter-productive to achieving your stated goal. And, it will likely set off that third voice which is the one saying you must not be meant to be an author, or you don't have what it takes to be a writer, otherwise you've have chosen the *should* action over the *want* action.

So, you need a way to see the process to reaching the goal in a different light. I'll give you two quite different approaches.

1. From SMART goals to joyful goals

Most of us aspire to be smart. From our first days in elementary school, the children who did well on quizzes were given positive attention from the teacher and had gold stickers put on their work. Who doesn't love a gold sticker? For some kids, that smart, gold-star work was then hung on the fridge so others would see and congratulate them. And so, they quickly developed a desire to be associated with this word, "smart."

But when you're setting your writing goals, I want you to consider not being smart. Well, not being SMART.

For most of my career I was an almost cult-like cheerleader for setting SMART goals. Between 1998 and 2016, I taught the SMART goal-setting approach to thousands of staff and volunteers of not-for-profit organizations and to hundreds of individuals in financial literacy courses.

I used to think that any goal that wasn't SMART, was dumb. And then... I started to coach writers and facilitate mastermind groups. That's when my beloved SMART goal approach started to show its imperfections. For the first time I got to watch the full process, from the moment the goal was set through 12-weeks of implementation.

Following along as writers created their beautifully Specific, Measurable, Attainable, Results-oriented, and Time-bound goals for our 12 weeks together, and checking-in on progress every two weeks, was eye-opening.

I watched and engaged in a process that included disappointment and frustration as bi-weekly mini-goals were often missed. Progress was being made, but when a stated goal wasn't 100% reached, rather than seeing the success of the work they had done, these writers often felt like they'd failed.

It became clear that the language around goal-setting was part of the problem. It's filled with absolutes and commands. Goal-setting has the voice of a Drill Sergeant in an army.

> "Troops! Up at 6:00. Write those words before work. You've got 45 days to get that story finished. I don't care if your fingers are bleeding. Write! Write! Write!"

If that's not bad enough, laying on the ground in front of the Sergeant is a recruit who was enlisted by his father and who has no desire to be part of the training. He whispers, loud enough for you to hear, things like,

> "I'm not good enough. My story is boring. Every other writer has tougher finger tips than I do. I can't do this."

For the majority of us, neither of these SMART-goal-bred voices are very helpful.

But it wasn't just the commanding tone of the goals that were the problem. Even writers who made great progress were arriving at the meetings apologizing to the group for having failed to meet their intended goals. So even if they'd written 5000 new words, if they'd set a goal to write 6000 new words, the achievement was tainted by a feeling of failure. And that feeling picked away at their motivation and self-confidence.

Of course, this was not how I wanted my beloved writers to feel during our meetings. I wanted them to feel like winners, to arrive in our meetings saying, "That was a great week," and to leave knowing that the next two weeks would give them more opportunities to feel positive about their work-in-progress. In a moment of inspiration, at the end of one meeting, my inner unicorn hip-checked my inner Drill Sergeant and rather than asking participants to complete the sentence, "In the next two weeks I commit to [goal achievements]," I asked them to finish this sentence,

"In the next two weeks it would bring me joy to …"

And don't you know that at our next check-in people's energy was upbeat. They reported on what they'd gotten done. If someone had said, "It would bring me joy to edit three chapters of my story" and came back having edited two chapters, there was no longer that feeling of having failed to meet a commitment, there was rather a feeling of success and statements like, "I'd hoped to get three chapters edited, but I got two chapters done and I'm happy with that."

Writer after writer reported in on their successes, rather than where they fell short. I still had to remind folks to not use words like "only" and "just" but overall, the tone was much more positive.

How can changing one word in a goal-setting statement make such a difference? In a word, dopamine. In a neuroscientific explanation, it's the habenula at work.

The habenula is a part of our brain's limbic system and it plays a role in motivation and mood. Give it something to celebrate and it releases the feel-good hormone dopamine. But feed it failure and it will starve us of the good feels and send a message to, "Run Away!" Literally, it will send a message to our brain to avoid that action.

In a blog post called, "The Power of Process," Dr. Kyra Bobinet, the author of *Well Designed Life*, writes of the habenula,

> "This useful tool is thought to keep us from wasting our time (or endangering ourselves) by repeating unsuccessful behaviors. When we measure goals in terms of success or failure, and then don't 'succeed,' the habenula kills our incentive to give things another go. This keeps a lot of dieters, would-be novelists, and aspiring entrepreneurs stuck at square one."

So, do I now avoid SMART goal-setting? Not at all. I still believe there's an important role for SMART (and the even better SMARTER goals, which add on E for Exciting and R for Rewarded or Risky, depending on your personality) to the process of completing a scrappy rough draft and beyond that, getting that manuscript through all the steps on the path to publication.

The SMART(ER) goal is long-term. The SMART(ER) goal is a state of completion. But the process of getting there does not include setting even more mini-SMART(ER) goals with their dopamine-killing commitments, it focuses on identifying ways to trigger the dopamine-*producing* habenula with little wins, actions and successes that bring us joy.

2. From goal-setting to directional planning

Are you someone who enjoys the journey as much as, or even more than, reaching the destination? I'm like that. When I go hiking, I find joy in stopping to smell the fir trees and to look in rivers and over cliffs. I'm the type of person who focuses on the process. My husband, however, is all about getting to the spot he has in mind, our end-point is his goal. For him, the joy of the hike is reaching the goal; for me it's how we get there.

It's no surprise that traditional, SMART goal-setting works well for my litigation manager husband and that my creative self has better luck using directional planning to set my path.

Management researchers in the 1970s determined that focusing on your *domain* and *direction* is an effective way to beat that goal-failure circle some people encounter. Michael McCaskey of the Harvard Business School studied this different approach in his paper called *Goals and Direction in Personal Planning*.

"Domain is the area in which one wants to operate... A person's choice of domain marks his or her boundaries for action and commitment.

"Direction is a symbolic expression of who one wants to become...Determining direction is built upon self-examination and an individual's deep sense of who he or she is."

Another way to think about domain and direction is to consider the questions one answers in determining them. Creating and choosing a domain answers the question,

- "What do you want to do? In the shifting field of choice and obligation, what territory do you want to mark out?"

Determining direction can be done by answering the question,

- "Who am I?" several times.

One of the main differences between goal-setting and directional planning is the focus on allowing the end-point to be less clear at the start of the process. Directional planning relies on an adaptive and iterative approach to the work you're doing and that allows you to learn along the way and to change your original plans without feeling like you've made a mistake or done something wrong.

According to the researchers, people who fit the Myers-Briggs personality type of sensation-thinking are more comfortable and successful using traditional goal-setting, while those who are feeling and intuition personality types are better-suited to use the domain and direction model.

For more information about Myers-Briggs personality types—and how you can use them to develop more interesting characters in your scrappy rough draft—have a look at Eileen Cook's book in this Creative Academy Guides for Writers series called, *Build Better Characters*.

Your Turn

Exercise 1: Set joy-filled SMART goals

If you've set yourself a goal (SMART, SMARTER, or otherwise) with a completion date, write that goal and date at the top of a page. I suspect it will be phrased something like,

- I will complete 65,000 words of the scrappy rough draft of [my book's working title] by [a reasonable date].

Assuming your current word count is less than half your target and your end date is more than a few weeks out, consider all the pieces that you still need to bring together to reach that goal. This is more than just word count (since it's hard to find joy in math) so think in terms of the creative steps that need to be tackled. For instance,

- Finish the research on how ancient miners in Greece moved rocks out of underground mines.
- Plan the major plot points for the middle of the story.
- Write a list of ten ways my heroine will try to kill the bad guy.

Now, using a calendar that matches your timeline, fill in tasks that it will bring you joy to get done. It might look like this:

- Week 1: It will bring me joy to know how my heroine is carrying ore out of the mine.
- Week 2: It will bring me joy to be clear on what happens at Turning Point TP#1 (the opportunity), TP#2 (change of plans), TP#3 (point of no return), TP#4 (major setback), and TP#5 (climax).
- Week 3: It will bring me joy to write three scenes in which my heroine takes down three different bad guys using three different approaches.

The point here is really to find a way to love the process of achieving mini-goals without triggering the dark side of the habenula when you miss a day or a week of writing.

For instance, feel the difference between these two statements, assuming you were not able to solve the plot challenge in the exact time you'd set as your mini-goal:

"This week, I commit to figuring out how to get my hero out of jail" versus

"This week, it will bring me joy to figure out how my hero gets out of jail."

In the first instance, if it takes you ten days to realize your hero will be saved by a cell phone video that shows he's innocent, odds are you'll have spent at least a couple of days upset that you'd not met your commitment to yourself—and your poor hero. No dopamine for you!

But, framed as a solution that you'll find joy in figuring out, even if the cell phone video doesn't show up "on time," you've created a situation where dopamine will be released when you do get the answer. Hooray.

Better still, your motivation to figure out your next scrappy rough draft challenge will be higher than if you'd framed this goal as a commitment you'd not met.

Focus on the joy that accompanies the completion of your writing tasks and see how that changes how you feel about your progress.

Exercise 2: Figure out your author domain

Let's assume that you already know that one of the ways you answer the question, "Who am I?" is, "I am a writer," or "I am an author."

While thinking about the fact that you are a writer/author, answer these two domain questions,

- "What do you want to do?"
- "What writing/author territory do you want to mark out?"

Exercise 3: Picture your author future

If you want to break free from the logical, analytical approach to answering the questions above, create a collage with images of symbols, the kind of energy, emotions, and interests that represent your writing domain.

If you have access to magazines, cut and paste. If not, Google and Canva.com are your friends. Find images that resonate with your inner writer and paste them together into a picture of future author you. Add words that have meaning. And then, save the image as a screensaver or print it out and hang it in your writing area.

Other techniques to create an image of your author future which can help keep you motivated to achieve that vision include keeping a dream journal, writing your obituary, and making a list of book or movie characters you identify with.

15

HOW TO DEVELOP 'FRESH START' BEHAVIOURS

"How long will you put off what you are capable of doing just to continue what you are comfortable doing?" ~James Clear

It took me almost ten full years from the day I wrote the first words of my first fiction manuscript to the day I held that book in my hands. Ten years. It's a long time to be thinking about, but only sometimes working on, an important project.

We know from all kinds of research that the more times we say we're going to achieve a goal—lose weight, get a new job, write our first book—and then fail to follow through, the less likely it is that the next time we make that declaration, that we'll be successful.

This has to do with our minds knowing we've already tried and failed and sending us subtle messages that we've already proven we're not going to succeed, so, why bother trying again? We don't like to fail. Don't make us fail again. This half-assed try and then fail pattern also teaches us that we can't trust the promises we make to ourselves.

You know how it feels when a friend who's let you down, stood you up several times before, says that she'll meet you, for sure on-time, this time? You may try to feel confident in her, but inside you're preparing to be having coffee on your own. Right?

That's what we start to do with our own commitment to ourselves.

Back to my story. My book was published three weeks before I turned fifty. Now that was not a coincidence, it was 100% by design. I started to write the novel that morphed into *Mother Teresa's Advice for Jilted Lovers* when I was forty. I decided then that I was going to write a book and have it published. So, although I'd written two novels by the time I was 49 years old, I was sitting on them. Scared to share them. Seriously, terrified that people would hate my story and therefore hate me. But being on the brink of turning fifty, a significant milestone age, gave me the motivation I needed to push past that fear.

In the months after I self-published my book, I started to realize that I've been motivated to act on big changes in my life at several milestone dates. So, I did some research to see if my experience was the norm or unique. Well, I can tell you that I am not a special snowflake, that my experience of using that change of decades is a very common milestone to motivate action.

Milestones help us achieve goals because they highlight the gap between our current behaviour and our desired future behaviour. That is what all the research has pointed towards.

This distinction between our past or current behaviour and our desired future behaviour gives us the opportunity to "wipe the slate clean." It gives us the authority to say, "That was then, this is now."

Our behaviour *before* the milestone we can assign to our past self. How we behave *after* the milestone is our current, and better self. This is why researchers call the milestone phenomenon, the **fresh start effect**.

These milestones dates create a new mental accounting period in your life. They let you—sometimes force you—to see your old self as the person who existed before that milestone day and to see your new self as a better, more focused version of that now-in-the-history-books, version of you.

It's powerful stuff.

Think about yourself ten years ago. The good, the bad, the ugly, the unimpressive, the spectacular…

Have you got something in your mind? I suspect you were able to come up with a few images in your mind's eye of that former version of yourself. It's a person you are not anymore.

Milestone and fresh start effect researchers have also found that we tend to compare our past self and our current self in ways that always allow us to maintain a positive, current self-view. For most of us, we'll leave our negative traits and failings with our past self when comparing who we are now to who we were then.

This is a fantastic tool to help us achieve goals since we can literally trick our brains into believing that some of the unproductive behaviours we're engaged in today can tomorrow be the behaviours of our past self.

It's not that hard to find examples of times we've done this. We decide to stop drinking, smoking, eating dessert, or binging on Netflix. We wake up, typically after reaching a breaking point with our behaviour, and say, "I used to waste an hour a day playing Scrabble on my phone, today and moving forward I am using my commuting time productively on my story."

And we do. We stop the behaviour that no longer brings us joy. And while we're passing on the ice cream, we're clear that "dessert eater" is one of our past selves, not our current self. The same is true on the positive side—going to yoga, buying more fresh potatoes than chips, and opening our manuscript instead of Facebook.

Odds are high that to write your book, you're going to need to change a habit or two. These will be your fresh start behaviours. And reading this book can be your milestone, the event on which you hang that break between your past self who hasn't been able to write their book, and your future self who is a published author.

Something to think about as you're reading is whether or not you have a change in your regular routine coming up soon. For instance, will you be going on vacation, starting a new job, or starting or finishing school? It's often easiest to form a new habit, make a fresh start in one area of your life, when you're having to change existing habits in another area.

Now, if you're anything like a typical human being, you've succeeded with behaviour change for periods of time and then gone back to your old behaviour. Unfortunately, most of us fail to see the great success in maintaining a productive habit for a set period of time once we fall back to our old habits. Which happens. We see that as a failure when, in fact, it was a big success to quit smoking for six months. To stop drinking while you were pregnant. To eat a ketogenic diet for four months to regain your health. Rather, we tend to focus on the fact that at Christmas we ate what was offered and had wine with dinner, then slowly fell back into our old eating and drinking patterns.

But there's one thing wrong with this thinking, especially as it applies your purpose right now of making the commitment to complete your scrappy rough draft.

A habit change that helps us achieve a goal does not have to be for your entire life to qualify it as a successful change. You decided to lose ten pounds so your wedding dress would fit in a particular way. You lost the ten pounds, got married at that wedding-day, goal-weight, and then you gained the weight back. You were 100% successful in achieving your goal. And yet, so many people feel like they failed when that weight comes back. That's not a fail, that's changing the goal line after your success.

It's time to recognize the times you've achieved a goal and then changed the goal line. That same drive that helped you lose ten pounds, quit drinking, or take Candy Crush off your phone is the source you'll be drawing on to get your book written.

I hope that you're feeling an amount of good about yourself and all your past successes right now.

Your Turn

The first exercise will have you capturing one bad habit you've quit, why you gave it up, and how it felt at the time you achieved that goal. Then the second exercise is like the flip side of that success coin, to help remember and write down a positive habit you've developed, why you started it, how it felt to succeed.

These two successes may have been a short-term habit you quit and a new habit you had but no longer engage in—the not-forever habit adjustments can still be resounding successes. And the reason I'm having you start here is so that your brain, your conscious mind, remembers these successes so it will trust that you can do it again. Once you've decided that writing your book is as important a goal as the ones you've identified, it can be a huge boost to your success.

Exercise 1: What bad habits have you given up?

Write down one bad habit you've had and given up, even just for a while. Write down what motivated you to give up that habit and how it feels or felt to succeed.

- Habit I gave up
- Why I gave it up
- How it felt to succeed

Exercise 2: What positive habits have you developed?

Write down one positive habit you've brought into your life, even just for a while. Write down what motivated you to start that habit and how it feels or felt to succeed.

- Habit I started
- Why I started
- How it felt to succeed

Exercise 3: What writing habits do you need to develop?

The next exercise will help you identify the writing habits that you feel would help you achieve your book-writing goal since books don't get written unless you make it a habit to actually write the words.

List the most important habits that you believe will allow you to achieve your writing goal. Here are a few common habits of published authors. In a notebook, elaborate on the ones that feel important to you.

1. Write regularly and meet your weekly writing targets

- Daily or weekly word count?
- Hours at the keyboard? Be specific.

2. Create a work environment that allows you to focus

- Comfy desk/chair set-up
- No pings, dings or rings
- Empty bladder, full mug/glass

3. Read books in the genre you're writing

- Bestsellers
- Favourite authors
- A recommendation from a librarian

4. Read craft books and blogs, listen to podcasts and take courses to support your development in areas you know your writing needs improvement

- Search Amazon and Goodreads for book ideas
- Search player.fm for podcasts about writing

5. Your own ideas

- Don't dismiss what your intuition tells you. It could be to develop a habit of writing in a coffee shop every morning or your car after work… if you think it could help, write it down.

Exercise 4: What habits does your gut tell you you should give up?

Next up you need to figure out which unproductive habit you could let go of to make time to have that space to succeed with your newly identified writing habit.

It may feel hard to put this down in black and white, but that's what you need to do. Write down the habit or behaviour you will quit in service of finishing your scrappy rough draft. (You can reinstall that game on your phone once your book is done!)

Exercise 5: What small action can you take right now?

If the habit you know you have to give up to make space to write is related to an app or technology, remove it right now. Immediately.

If the habit involves another person, set a time to talk to them about it and ask for their support in helping you give up the behaviour that's contributing to your book not getting done.

If it's something else, you know what you need to do. Now do it! Seriously. Do it.

Exercise 6: Create a new writing habit

This last exercise will help you to more clearly define your Fresh Start writing habit behaviours. It will take some time to think this through but doing the exercise thoughtfully could save you months or years of waffling.

1. Set a writing habit goal

Tips for defining your new writing habit:

1. Make it so small you know you can easily achieve or exceed it
2. State it in a short, specific statement

For example:

I will write for 15 minutes every day.

2. Set a trigger condition

Connect this new habit to a habit you already have that you never (or very rarely) deviate from, like brushing your teeth or reading in bed… Now connect it to the newly stated goal:

After I wash the dinner dishes
I will write for 15 minutes

3. Identify a reward

Identify a simple reward that you will give yourself each time you complete your writing goal. This reward should be one that you can have immediately—not a promise of a holiday in weeks or months. The reward also needs to be real, not simply a thought. Make the reward something physical, like dancing for three minutes or eating a piece of chocolate.

After I wash the dinner dishes, I will write for 15 minutes
then reward my commitment with one piece of chocolate.

4. Commit to act

Be explicit with yourself about why you will become a person who can unconditionally call themselves an author by completing the following sentence:

When <insert your trigger condition>, I will <insert your

writing habit goal> because I am the type of person who <finish the sentence>. For example,

> *When I finish washing the dinner dishes I will sit at my desk and work on my story for fifteen minutes…*
>
> *…because I am the type of person who keeps my promises.*
>
> *…because I am the type of person who values carving out time to do what I love.*
>
> *…because I am the type of person who believes that stories— including my own!—have the power to do good.*

Now that you've got your new habit figured out there's one last step, because having a daily habit that you can *always* fit in is a nice dream. Missing a day (or two or three) is 100% fine—as long as you commit to catch up those minutes or words in the week, or perhaps month if you have a longer timeframe for completion.

Some writers find it helpful to have a visual of their progress. Here are two different but effective approaches you could use to create your own personal accountability tracker until your writing has become a habit that you know you'll do.

MY GOAL: 5,000 words a week for 10 weeks (50,000 words total)

You can create your own spreadsheets or **download one from our creativeacademyforwriters.com/resources page.**

Shade in your daily word counts for each week. Here's how it might look after 4 weeks.

Day/Week		500	1000	1500	2000	2500	3000	3500	4000	4500	5000	5500	6000
Week 1													
Week 2													
Week 3													
Week 4													

MY GOAL: 30 minutes a day (15 total hours in the month)

In this model you mark off the writing blocks until you've reached—or to ensure you reach!—your target of fifteen hours in the month. The actual days on which you write the words is irrelevant.

Here's how it would look once you've written for 6 hours and 45 minutes.

Minutes		15	15	15	15	15	15	15	15	15	15	15	15
3 hours													
6 hours													
9 hours													
12 hours													
15 hours													

16

IF YOU DON'T KNOW WHERE/HOW
TO START

The purpose of the first draft is to discover. Peter Drucker calls it a "zero draft." Other names might be a trial draft, a test draft, a dress rehearsal draft, a practice draft, an explanation or an experimental draft. ~Donald Murray

I provide free, 30-minute coaching calls to writers who may be interested in working with me. Prior to any call I ask these writers to answer a few questions so I can get to know them and where they are in their writing process before our short time together. I tell people not to fuss over grammar or complete sentences, to simply write what comes to mind, that their answers will not be graded or judged.

My secret to making that thirty minutes valuable to whoever I'm meeting is these two simple questions:

1. What is the story or book you're struggling with?

2. What's been keeping you from working on it?

Now, I don't know how long it takes the average person to write their top-of-mind answers about their book, but I can tell you that these blurbs are usually a bit amorphous and vague.

> *"It's a memoir. Or maybe fiction? Or perhaps gonzo journalism? I'm not sure. But it's about girls who get themselves in trouble. And I don't just mean in the euphemistic way of "up the creek without a paddle" if you know what I mean, I mean in all the ways we get into trouble just for being a woman."*

(And that's my own example of a book idea that lived inside me for almost a decade, brewing and stewing and sneaking little bits of itself into lots of different projects).

I read the writer's summary statement and am always able to find questions, begging to be answered, embedded in their descriptions. I ask the what's, the why's, and the how's. And you know what? Virtually every writer can wax poetic about their idea. They can speak to the bones of their story with no trouble at all, even if they aren't able to articulate it in writing. Yet.

Often what I hear, once they've told me about their work-in-progress is a frustrated plea,

"But I just don't know where to start."

For me, who has only thirty minutes to help that writer make even one step toward their goal, this is the best question ever because they've described enough of their story—be it fiction or non-fiction—for me to have something to reflect back.

"Just write the story you just told me. That's your starting place. Maybe each sentence becomes a header that might turn into a scene or even a whole chapter, at least for now, in your scrappy rough draft."

The point is to get the ideas out from banging around inside your head. To see them on the monitor or page. To make them real.

Your Turn

You have an idea for a story. It doesn't matter how vague, write the idea down in as much detail as you can in two minutes. Write like nobody is reading—because nobody other than you will read this.

Once you have that broad description down, take a sentence—any sentence—and dig deeper by asking yourself a few questions: How? Why? What? Where? Who? When? You won't be able to answer all the questions, but you don't need to. You simply need to start to write into the story.

For instance, let's say in your brief story description you've written the line,

> *A young woman discovers she has a superpower that allows her to 'nudge' people to tell the truth when they're lying to her.*

Take that line and write—call it your zero draft if you don't feel like this is worthy of first draft—by answering some 'obvious' questions:

How did she discover her power?

- Write that scene.

Why does she want to figure out how to hone this power?

- Write that scene.

What job does she have that makes this a useful power?

- Write notes about her job.

Who does she nudge?

- Make a list of the kinds of people she wants the truth from.

Once you've done a few of these scenes and lists, you don't have to worry that you don't know how or where to start your scrappy rough draft… because you already have.

17

YOU CAN TELL A STORY 100 WAYS

"Nothing is perfect, nothing lasts, nothing is finished…Writing is an exercise in polishing a beautiful stone of perception."
~Richard R. Powell

The first thing I wrote in starting this particular book was an introduction. It was good enough for a scrappy rough draft, so I moved on to another section. After a few days, I decided that my first introduction wasn't quite right. So, I wrote another. And it was fine. For a few days.

I carried on with new sections, adding words to my work-in-progress. And writing new introductions. By the end of my third week working on this very book, I had written the introduction six times. Each time was a little different. In some ways it was a little better, in other ways, still not quite what I—or you—needed as your handshake into my pages.

Before I finished the draft, I was speaking with a new coaching client. She'd been making starts on her memoir for a few years and realized that she'd probably never finish it unless she had both accountability and someone to help her recognize the power of her story as she was working on her scrappy rough draft.

I gave her homework that first week, to simply outline all of the stories that were connected to the theme of her memoir. She did that easily and then started to write, like me, with an introduction. When we spoke the following week, she was stressed out that she'd written four entirely different introductions to her own life story.

"That's fantastic," I said.

"But I can't use four introductions," she argued.

"You already have," I countered. "How many words did you write in the last week?"

"8,000."

"And how many words did you write in the previous six months?"

"Not that many," she said.

"Congratulations! Now, set all the introductions aside. Don't worry where they end up in your memoir, or if they make the cut at all. You're writing yourself into the story that you need to tell. Well done."

The experience that she and I share, of not knowing exactly

where to start, is totally normal—especially if you're the kind of writer who doesn't start with an outline.

There is no right or wrong way to start. The type of writer you are, plotter, pantser, or planster (say that three times fast) largely depends on your personality. Try as I may, I will at best be a planster since I cannot see where I'm going until I'm already on the path.

So, if you're like me and likely half of all writers, you may find yourself writing and rewriting scenes or chapters while working on your scrappy rough draft as you figure out where your story and characters are headed. Just know that that's okay.

Eileen Cook, my own developmental editor and co-instructor in The Creative Academy has worked with hundreds of fiction writers over the years. She says,

> "I often suggest to writers that their story *really* starts on page 20 or chapter three. They needed to write those words to get into the story, but when it comes time for revision, they can often cut the opening."

The truth is that there are at least one hundred ways to tell a story. Think about the fact that there are really only seven distinct plots, according to Christopher Booker. What he means is that we have story tropes and those tropes lead readers to expect certain things in certain genres.

Take romance for instance. In traditional romance, you have the main story plot of girl meets boy (or girl meets girl, or boy meets boy). One wants a relationship but the other hesitates. Something happens to throw them together. Something else tears them apart. Another thing happens to show them they're meant for each other. They kiss and live happily ever after—at least for now.

As you get started writing your scrappy rough draft, you may or may not know the best way to bring those two characters together. So, you create a situation. And you keep writing. Then you realize your hero is terrified of heights so he couldn't have met his love interest skydiving —and you go back to rewrite that meeting scene. You carry on with your story and... darn it all, your heroine tells you that she's deadly allergic to garlic so the romantic dinner she and the hero had in an Italian restaurant falls apart. Fine. You put them in a Japanese restaurant instead.

The point is that even if you're a plotter you will likely run into places in your story while you're writing this first draft that won't work the way you planned or expected by the time you've reached the middle of your story.

And what you need to know is that you should both plan and expect this to happen so when it does, you can take a deep breath, make a note where you need to go back and make a change, then carry on writing.

The manuscript that I'd titled *Drinking Scotch With Strangers* was my first foray into fiction. My scrappiest rough draft was written in the first-person narrative but then I worried that it should have been written in third-person so I wrote it again. Then I read it in third-person and realized that first-person was better. I started again and wrote my third draft in first-person. At that point the manuscript was 120,000 words long. By the time an editor was done making suggestions for the bits that didn't belong in it, the fourth draft was just 60,000 words. (But thankfully still in first-person!)

And, by the time I was done with that version, I'd taken the main character and theme from the story and written something entirely different which is what became *Mother Teresa's Advice for Jilted Lovers*.

My scrappy rough draft, written by the seat of my pants, morphed and grew and shrunk and morphed again. The interesting thing is that although ninety percent of the story changed from my first scrappy rough draft to the book that is published, the one constant was the inciting incident, the moment that kicked off the action. But from there... finding the story arc was a long, sometimes painful process.

But writing *is* a process.

Your Turn

If you're not sure where your story starts and you're not interested in creating an outline, my tip is quite simple: just write.

Write knowing that you won't keep all the words. And that moving entire scenes to a "maybe in another book" folder is both normal and necessary. You and your story are getting to know each other—and you may still be in that stage at the end of your second or even third revision. It's all good. It's all normal. It's all part of the process of writing your book and especially writing your scrappy rough draft.

Even if you're a plotter who's created a multi-page outline, remind yourself that it's simply a guide. You can change the guide.

If you're at the stage in your scrappy rough draft where you're still not sure where your story starts, set your timer for fifteen minutes, open a notebook and write to complete the following phrase,

"Today I want to write about…".

What you write could be words in your manuscript, a scene that may or may not be at the beginning, a blog post you may or may not use to help promote your book… just let yourself write.

And be of good cheer. Love the words you're with right now. And when you tire of them or they of you, thank them for their company and unceremoniously move them to your draft file, to perhaps reunite with later.

18

PICK ONE FOCUS AND STICK WITH IT

"Every hour you spend writing is an hour you spent not fretting about your writing." ~Dennis Palumbo

I don't know if it's my age, the fact I'm a woman, the way my brain works, or a my level of self-awareness, but I am a terrible multitasker. Like, so bad that I cannot wash the dishes and talk about the weather at the same time.

Before my son moved away he had a large desk set up in the family room where he'd do most everything a young man in university does. To achieve his goals, he had three monitors connected to his computer. In fact, one of the monitors was actually a 30-inch television. He wasn't using the three monitors as a contiguous screen—he had whatever he was reading for university on one monitor, a video game he was actively playing on another, and the third was either streaming someone else playing a game or had some Netflix show on it.

It drove me crazy. No matter how many times I told him that he couldn't possibly do well on any of the tasks with his focus so diluted, he'd argue that I shouldn't impose my slower-processing brain power onto his much more competent grey matter.

At the time I didn't have science to back me up but I had lots of anecdotal evidence from participants in my *Book On Fire* course and the mastermind groups I've led, that having more than one writing project vying for your attention makes getting anything done on any of the projects especially difficult.

Now I *do* have the science, or a name for the challenge that humans (all humans, not just women of a certain age) face when we try to multi-task. Motivation scientists call it **behavioural chatter**, the flitting from one goal to another without making significant progress on any particular one. Clearly, this is something we'd like to avoid. This is something we *need* to avoid to complete that first draft of our manuscript.

In my writing world (that space in my head) I typically have at least one client project (technical writing, not very creative), one fiction story, a non-fiction book, and several creative non-fiction short pieces vying for my attention in any given week.

And when I'm thinking about all or even two of those projects at once, none get my best attention, focus, or words. For instance, when I agreed to write a book in the Creative Academy Guides for Writers series, I was about four months into being (almost) solely focused on a full-length book that I'd done hundreds of hours of research on and had managed to write about 15,000 scrappy rough draft words for. The only way I could manage writing the book that you're reading right now was to put that other one aside.

Having multiple projects is fabulous. Having a diluted focus is a problem.

The trick is really to figure out which of your projects is most in-need of your attention *right now*—the one that is demanding you pay attention to it, like the chocolate chips in the cupboard that are begging to be made into cookies. While it may feel like picking one of your book babies over the others would be like declaring which of your children you love the best, there is a simple way to help you figure that out. (The book you should be focusing on; not which child you love most).

If you're not clear which of your books or stories you're going to give your attention to in the immediate future, you'll continue to think about all of them. And, when you sit down to write, you'll likely spend some amount of time debating which of your projects you'll work on. Once you decide, your mind will still be focused to a degree on your other stories. It makes it difficult to fall into that space where you get lost in your own story.

One way to eliminate, or at least reduce the behavioural chatter, is to make a list of all the books, stories, and ideas that you have that you'd like to write about, assign a unique letter to each project, and then prioritize them.

For instance, my list recently looked like this:

A — Scrappy Rough Draft (50,000 word how-to)

B — The Unholy Communion of Sex, Religion, and Politics (100,000 word creative non-fiction)

C — Short non-fiction piece for the CBC contest (2500 words)

D — Daily post for Medium.com (500 to 2000 words each)

E — Client project on financial literacy topic (25,000 words)

F — *WordWorks* magazine story pitch (750 words)

G — Untitled women's fiction with 20,000 words written

H — Choose your own ending story (100,000 words)

I — Random writing for The Creative Academy

Can you see how, if I didn't prioritize each of these works-in-progress, my brain and I would be more likely to walk away from the desk to take a nap than to sit down and give my attention to my writing? It's overwhelming to have that many projects vying for your attention.

The next step of this exercise is to compare pairs of projects in the order you wrote them down and decide which of the two projects "wins" right now—and for a defined period of time ahead, say one week or until the chosen project is complete.

So, I would consider A—Scrappy Rough Draft vs B—The Unholy Communion and see if one of the two projects is a clear winner of my most immediate time. In the case of these two, it was an easy decision since both projects are equally fun to research and write (and fun for me is important in my creative work), but *Scrappy Rough Draft* had a clear due date. The Unholy Communion had no external deadlines so, it was bumped for now.

My own project C—Short non-fiction piece for the CBC contest, had a due date almost three full months from the date I made the list and that date was after this book was intended to be published. Easy choice. Project C can be safely put to my list of Work on Later projects.

And so on. The only one that caused some consternation was the article I wanted to pitch to *WordWorks* magazine. Although the piece was short, only 750 words, I knew that it would take me at least eight hours to do the research, write and polish the piece. That was too much time given my immediate, immovable deadlines. The magazine publishes four times a year, so I decided to send my pitch for the next issue. No guilt and no busy mind-chatter taking up important space that this book and the client project needed right now.

Your Turn

Write each of your projects on its own sheet of paper—you can tear the paper into four pieces first or use index cards if you have some.

For projects that have an external deadline, write that down too.

Determine the timeframe for your focus, be it a week, a couple of weeks or even a couple of months.

Compare projects in pairs until you've identified just one project (at most two) to focus on for the time period you've chosen.

If choosing is too difficult, consider the following criteria to help you determine the priority of each of your writing projects:

1. What is the most important project?

You define "important" in whatever way makes sense to you. For instance if you'll be pitching your manuscript to agents or editors at an upcoming conference and hope to be asked to submit, this could be your most important project to focus on. A contest deadline might also give a project 'Most Important' status.

2. What project is closest to being done?

It may be work you're not excited to do, but eliminating projects that you can wrap up and move along frees mental space—and makes room to add new projects. For instance, a project that just needs you to run it through Grammarly or ProWriting Aid so you can send it to beta readers.

3. What is the easiest project?

Completing the easiest project will give you a win and that can boost your confidence as you move into the next project on your list.

4. What is the oldest project?

Is the idea still important to you? Still relevant? Will it

continue to be? Sometimes a project will sit so long it becomes too stale to bother completing.

5. What project do you wake up thinking about—in a happy way, not with a shadow of guilt?

Sometimes, especially when none of our projects have external deadlines and we've been struggling to put bum in chair, consciously deciding to work on the project that is the most fun is a good way to get us back into the habit of writing.

Place the papers that represent the projects you're *not* working on right now in a place you can find them so that when you're ready to pick up another project, you'll have these ready to review. This saves you time since you won't need to make new cards, *and* it gives your brain the confidence to '"forget" about them for now.

19

HOW TO USE A CARROT AS A STICK TO MEET WRITING TARGETS

"Being decisive is itself a choice. Decisiveness is a way of behaving, not an inherited trait. It allows us to make brave and confident choices, not because we know we'll be right, but because it's better to try and fail than to delay and regret. Our decisions will never be perfect, but they can be better. Bolder. Wiser. The right process can steer us toward the right choice."
~Dan and Chip Heath

A couple of years ago I was researching the power of embracing the **fresh start effect** to help achieve life milestones. Researchers pointed to a website that was created for people who know that promising themselves nice things when they reach their goals (carrots) will *not* help keep them motivated. This website works by promising the opposite:

If you *fail* to meet your goal, you must pay real money to a not-for-profit organization that you *don't* support. You think of a group that has a mission that makes your face scrunch up, and you commit your money to them. But you only send it if you fail to meet your goal.

It's a neat idea but one that never resonated with me since I figured that if I missed my goal I'd simply lie to the app and say I achieved it to avoid sending my precious dollars to the NRA.

But there is an easy work-around, one you can use with a trusted friend or an accountability coach.

How it works: You set a measurable goal, for instance to write a certain number of words a day or week. You tell your accountability buddy what the goal is and then you report in with your proof of the written words (as scrappy as they may be since they aren't going to actually read them) on time. Every time.

Now, your accountability buddy has in their possession a stamped and addressed envelope to a charity that you absolutely do not want to donate money to. Inside that envelope is either a cheque or your credit details with a donation in an amount that would make you feel horrible if it found its way into the wrong hands. It could be as little as $50 or as much as $5,000. You know what would hurt. Write the amount for that much.

If you fail to meet your deadline, your accountability buddy has strict instructions to mail that envelope.

And that is how you turn a motivational carrot into a stick.

In the *Author on Fire Mastermind and Accountability* groups we host in The Creative Academy, members have created variations on this approach. When one writer was missing her goal of submitting queries to agents and knew that the only thing stopping her was fear, another member offered to be the recipient of both the carrot and the stick.

Here's what they did:

Member Two loves her chocolate but only eats it as a treat. She proposed to Member One a deal wherein she (Member Two) would get the benefit (the carrot) of success when Member One reported having sent five queries. It took a few days, but each day, with all of us asking if Member Two could have her treat yet, Member One pushed past her fear, got the queries sent and allowed our friend to have some chocolate.

After that successful experiment, another pair took the opposite approach. One member *gave up* her beloved chocolate until the first writer achieved a specific target that had been dogging her for weeks. She accepted the stick. We don't want to let people we like down, which is why this approach worked.

Your Turn

If you have the kind of personality that might benefit from this kind of motivation and accountability, find the friend who can provide the reason that you'll live up to your commitment to your writing and come up with a carrot/stick combination that's fun and will work for you.

SKULKING AROUND THE WRITER'S BLOCK

"Each time I sit down to write I don't know if I can do it. The flow of writing is always a surprise and a challenge. Click the computer on and I am 17 again, wanting to write and not knowing if I can." ~Donald Murray

Even once you've embraced the approach of allowing yourself to write a scrappy rough draft, odds are high that you'll have days when the words don't flow, days they feel hung-up, stuck, constipated. Dare I say, days when you and your writing feel shitty.

In other words, you'll still have days when you may feel inclined to believe that you have writer's block. Many authors poo-poo the idea that writer's block even exists, claiming that if a writer isn't writing, the problem is less like a block, something that stands in the way, and more akin to an absence of direction.

In the 80s and 90s, social scientists who studied creativity processes referred to blocks not as a physical thing (like a wall) but as a verb. They called it "blocking."' This is an interesting twist in the idea of what's taking place when we sit down to write but find ourselves unable to type words. Or worse, reach the hour we promised ourselves we'd sit down to write, and find a hundred-and-one reasons to avoid the chair.

I remember once reading that an author likens writer's block to seeing ghosts—the only people who experience the phenomenon are the ones who believe that ghosts exist. He or she chose not to believe in writer's block. They asserted that writer's block is simply a writer who is not writing. And that the way to *not* have writer's block is to put fingers on keyboard and write. That easy. So, they said.

I know the reality is more difficult than that, but I like this different way of thinking since it forces me to own my inaction. I can't point at the block and say, "Geez, sorry, that metaphorical mass is too big to push through so I guess I'll watch Netflix instead." Rather, if I'm *blocking* it means that I'm already undertaking an action. And if that's the case, there's no reason to continue my negative impact action when I could be engaging in a more productive action: writing.

In some ways, it *is* just that easy. Just like putting on sneakers is a simple act that any one of us can do, taking the next step of running five miles is not so easy. But having a clear understanding of why we block—whether it be with our writing or any other goal we've set—can go a long way in helping us figure out how not to block.

But before I explain what blocking is and what triggers it, I want to challenge you to consider something you've likely never considered: perhaps, if you're blocked while writing your first draft, that's *exactly* what's supposed to be happening for you and your story right now.

Dr. Donald Murray wrote an article in the early 80s called "The Essential Delay: When Writer's Block Isn't," in which he argues that there are points in every writer's manuscript when it's simply not the right time to be writing, that what we need to be doing is thinking. He says that we should stop worrying that when words don't flow that we may be blocking. That this pause is "the normal, necessary, always terrifying delay that precedes effective writing."

In Murray's treatise, he cites five things a writer needs to know—or feel—before writing.

- Information
- Insight
- Order
- Need
- Voice

The reason this is so important to have as a foundation for understanding your own blocking is because if you judge yourself and the time you're sitting at your desk, staring out the window, when you think your fingers should be flying across keys, you'll trigger a process in your brain system that can, and probably will, create an actual block to your ability to work on your manuscript.

Joseph LeDoux is a neuroscientist and the Director of the

Emotional Brain Institute. He researched the connection between brain science and the creative process and what he determined offers writers some helpful ideas about why writer's block can feel so insurmountable. It's all about the way two of the three parts of our brains work together.

Short biology or neuroscience lesson now (don't gloss over this as there will be a test):

Your brain has three main components: the stem, the cortex, and the amygdala (also known as the limbic system). We can ignore the stem since it's not playing a critical role in the way we respond to feeling blocked. When you're doing something creative, like writing a book, your cortex, which is your learning brain, is in charge. But, when your cortex gets a whiff of danger, the amygdala, your emotional brain, takes over.

We're not conscious of this hostile take-over. In fact, that sneaky, life-saving amygdala triggers our freeze, fight, flight process but does so with such stealth that after the spontaneous reaction, our cortex is already explaining why *it* acted the way *it* did. Our naïve cortex doesn't realize that it was the amygdala that made it trigger the action to have us jump away from the spider-shaped piece of fluff on the carpet—or the blank page on our monitor.

LeDoux described the relationship like being on a bus. Your cortex is in the driver's seat and doing a fine job. But something startles the sensitive cortex so the amygdala shoves the cortex to the back and takes control of the wheel. Meanwhile, the cortex still thinks it's in control, but the steering wheel in its hands is just a toy steering wheel like toddlers play with. Mr. Cortex is busy turning the (toy steering) wheel, but the bus is still driving straight ahead. What the heck? The cortex can't understand why the bus isn't moving in the direction it's trying to take it.

It's important to know what situations push your cortex out of the driver's seat since the amygdala doesn't care about your creative process or what your cortex was working on. Its only motivation is to keep you alive.

In many ways, this relationship between your cortex and your amygdala sounds a lot like what might drive the conversations between your normal, rational self (who knows you have a great story to tell) and your inner critic (who can only see all the reasons why writing your book is a bad idea).

Your inner critic (amygdala) is a control freak. Its only job is to save you from yourself. There's a whole section on quieting your inner critic in Chapter 10, cleverly titled, **The science of the inner critic**, but for now I want to focus on how and why your amygdala is likely playing a role in what many of us call writer's block. Then we'll tackle ways to give control back to your cortex, effectively, *unblocking*.

When your emotional brain detects a threat, it jumps into action. Now, that threat may be something real, like a tarantula crawling across your desk, or perceived, like the criticism you *could* receive when you share your story. Your amygdala does not discriminate. The unfortunate thing is that this lack of discrimination may also give rise to an amygdalic take-over when you have the should-be-benign thought, "Blech. This writing is crap. Nobody will want to read this."

Rationally, you know that it's fine to be writing unpublishable words in your scrappy rough draft, that you'll have time to rewrite and that your only job right now is to get the story out. Your first draft is the clay from which you'll sculpt your story. Or, to use an even more apt metaphor, the fruit (of your labour) grows better in shit than in air.

It's all fine and good to understand that you can't write when the wrong brain is at the keyboard, but simply knowing this doesn't mean the usurper will give up their position. You need some strategies to dethrone them. The following are ways that I and fellow writers have effectively used to help us stop blocking and get back to writing when we're at the desk, but not producing fertilizer for our manuscripts.

Your Turn

Exercise 1: Breathe

I cannot overemphasize the value of taking a few—or several—minutes to sit and breathe into your belly. Don't do that normal breathing that just fills the top of your lungs. That's not going to do the trick. What you need to do is take long, deep-to-your-belly breaths. The kind that will make you feel a bit dizzy if you do too many of them.

And here, I'll get a bit *woo woo* on you. I used to have a regular yoga practice. It was every Thursday evening from

7:00 to 8:15 PM. The yoga we did was in the Hatha tradition and there was a great deal of focus on our chakras and ensuring we were breathing deep into our root. I knew I felt good after yoga, but something became clear to me once I started working on the manuscript that became my first novel: I was at my most creative on Thursday nights. I'd get home from yoga feeling equally relaxed and energized. It was a remarkable thing. The words I wrote on Thursday came with an ease that I didn't have on other evenings that I wrote. At the time, I didn't understand why this was, but I went with it.

Understanding the state that my brain was in and that the yoga had effectively put my amygdala to sleep for the evening, I now know why those were my most productive writing sprints.

You don't need to downward dog to make it work for you. Just focus on your breathing if your words aren't flowing. Don't worry about the thoughts that pop up, just keep coming back to the focus on your breath. What you're doing is relaxing your limbic brain system and giving your body lots of oxygen—and that works like a charm to put your cortex back in charge so you can break the block.

Exercise 2: Adjust your expectations

Having mini-goals is good, except, when it's not. If you've set yourself a goal to write 1000 words in each writing session and you haven't achieved the goal—or, you typically miss the mark—you're creating stress. Stress is an invitation for your amygdala to take over since its only job is to keep you alive and it knows that stress is a killer.

There are ways to put your cortex back in control in this situation. You could reduce your word count goal to something lower than your typical writing sprint output. This will put you in a more positive frame of mind when you sit down to write. With an expectation of success, you won't feel stress so your amygdala won't be triggered to act. Result: no writer's block.

Or, you could drop counting words altogether and decide that you'll write one scene, or one dialogue exchange, or finish a chapter that you've been working on.

And finally, if neither of those ideas spark joy, set the goal to sit in your writing chair with your work in progress open (and all other distractions closed) for a set number of minutes. If you type words, great. If you close your eyes and imagine a scene from your story, wonderful. If you reread what you've already written without worrying about editing, fantastic. Those are all wins and can help your cortex find its rightful spot in your creative process again.

Exercise 3: Procrastinate productively

There's a whole section earlier in this book on how to be a productive procrastinator, but the quick how-to is simply to give your brain something to work on that relaxes you before you sit down to write. If you knit, pull out your needles. If you draw, grab your colour-makers of choice. If you love being in the kitchen, make some cookies (email me for my mailing address!).

This works because when you're doing something you love and have some skill with, your amygdala relaxes and stops trying to get involved. Once you've spent fifteen minutes engaged in an activity that allows your limbic brain to stand down there's a good chance you'll maintain control when you open your work-in-progress. Just do so without high expectations.

An interesting factoid about writer's block

Have you ever wondered where the term "writer's block" comes from? One of Sigmund Freud's disciples, an American psychoanalyst named Dr. Edmund Bergler coined the phrase in 1947, suggesting it was a psychological condition.

He said writer's block was one manifestation of psychic masochism, which is "the unconscious wish to defeat one's conscious aims, and to enjoy that self-constructed defeat." Some other manifestations that share the bed with writer's block, according to Dr. Bergler, are gambling, alcoholism, and kleptomania!

Think about that the next time you declare yourself to have this affliction... writer's block, I mean; not psychic masochism.

Want more from Dr. Bergler? I suggest finding, *The Writer and Psychoanalysis* (1950). It's an interesting read.

21

WHY IT'S IMPORTANT TO CELEBRATE SMALL WINS

"What do you care enough about that you're prepared to expose yourself to fear, risk and hard work to get?" ~Seth Godin

We've all heard the stories about authors who had stacks of rejections from agents and publishers before finding the one person who saw the potential in their book and then sold millions of copies. One of the most famous is from Jack Canfield, the author of the original *Chicken Soup for the Soul*. It took 144 rejections before a publisher gave the book a green light. Today there are over 250 titles in the Chicken Soup series which have sold over 100 million copies in Canada and the US alone.

Robert Pirsig had to endure 121 rejections before a publisher was willing to take a chance on *Zen and The Art of Motorcycle Maintenance*, which became a literary classic. Lisa Genova, who was either rejected or ignored by over 100 agents, decided to self-publish *Still Alice* and then a publisher made her an offer and that book spent forty weeks on the New York Times bestseller list. Kathryn Sockett received sixty agent rejections for *The Help* which went on to sell millions of copies and inspire a multi-award-winning film thanks to agent query #61.

So, what kept these authors querying agents and pitching publishers in the face of so much rejection? And how does this apply to you, a writer who's still working on your first draft and not yet close to starting your own illustrious rejection pile (assuming you're not going straight down the indie-publishing path)?

It is this:

Every one of those rejections was a small win for those authors, whether they felt that way or not in the moment (and odds are that they did not). They were wins because every time they sent their pages to another editor or agent, they were acting with courage and with the confidence that they'd written books worth reading.

Their faith in their books, even on the days when it was hard to have, is the big win. And this is where the lesson is for you, even at this early stage of the writing process.

Over the course of writing your book, you will face failures. It's inevitable. You'll set goals and fail to meet them. You'll write words that felt like poetry as they poured from your fingertips, only to read them later and realize they just don't work (at least not in the current book). You may lose files and spend days fretting that you'll never be able to write those scenes as well again. Well-meaning people will ask you the rudest question one can ask of a writer, "Are you *still* working on that same old book?" and it will make you feel like throwing the book at them...or maybe a whole truckload of books! There will be failures.

But you will also have wins. So many wins. You'll write 3,000 words in one day and it will be your personal best writing day. You'll write a turn of phrase that makes you feel all warm inside. You'll figure out the most wonderful, awful way to tear your lovers apart so that they can grow and come back together stronger. You'll solve story problems that haunt your sleep and drive you to drink green smoothies since you heard that those can fuel creativity. You'll finish a scene. And a chapter. And then another and another.

The problem with us—all of us—is that unless we make a conscious effort to acknowledge those achievements as wins, they get lost in all the noise. We discount them, saying things to ourselves like "It's just one scene. Big deal. I have to write a hundred more."

But it *is* a big deal. A deal big enough to celebrate— perhaps not with champagne *every* time, but with an actual act of acknowledgement. Because without that scene you'd not be able to write the next one. And the next. And the next.

There is science behind the act of celebrating small wins, too. Our brains are quick to remember all of the things that we haven't done well and then to tell ourselves that those failures are who we are in that area of our life.

As an example, I'll use myself and my parenting. When my son was in Grade Two, I sent him to school with an untreated broken arm. He'd been sledding the day before with friends in the school playground and had taken a tumble. He told me his arm hurt but to my eye it looked fine. He was still able to play his half-hour of video game before dinner, so I assumed it was just a bruise. We propped it on a pillow when he went to bed and he slept through the night. I packed him into his snowsuit, walked him to school the next day and left him in the fine care of his teacher—who called me an hour later. I can't tell you if the tone of his voice was judgement or bemusement, but there was a tone when he said, "Donna, you need to take Liam to the hospital. He has a broken arm." *Ouch*—and I mean to my self-confidence as a loving mother more than to my seven-year-old's sore arm.

That was one of those milestone moments in my parenting life.

As was the call I got when Liam was fifteen and away at a summer leadership camp. He'd been gone all of eight hours. My husband and I were planning to go on a motorcycle road trip, something we rarely got to do since no self-respecting teenager would ride in a sidecar with his parents. Liam had been playing a game of capture the flag and was tackled by the only kid at camp bigger than he was. He hit the ground and his arm was bent, at the elbow, in the wrong direction. He was waiting for an ambulance (which was hours away since leadership camps are always in remote areas, right?) and would be having surgery that night.

Our trip to get to him took several hours and involved a ferry, but we arrived just as he was coming out of his surgery. Being there for my son's second broken arm is a win that helped counter the 'failure' of how I handled his first. And all the bruises and cuts that he experienced between the two milestone moments? Forgotten. I'm sure that I kissed a good number of boo-boos over his childhood, but I remember none of them since they were just the normal things that a parent does in the day-to-day routine of raising a child.

From a brain science point of view, we are very good at remembering moments that leave us feeling bad and the major milestone events that bring us joy. But we're rubbish with keeping count of the small wins. And when you're writing a book, there are so few big wins that you have to acknowledge all of the small wins. Those small wins keep you fuelled up.

Rather than giving power to that voice that says: "Why do you think you can write a book? You've been trying for ten years and what have you got to show for it? Where is this so-called book?" your small wins give power to a different voice, the one that has legitimate answers to the Snarky-Pants Inner Critic.

That new voice can say, "Whoa, Nellie! I've written a kick-ass outline. Have you seen it? The way my main character transforms from a timid teen to the CEO of her own empire? Have you read the scene where she takes down the bank manager who refused to give her a business loan? Have you noticed that I've written over 10,000 words of this book, which means I'm at least 15% done this baby?!"

Small wins give us the motivation to keep working toward our big goals. But we have to *acknowledge* the small wins for them to be effective.

The science this is based on originates with Teresa Amabile and Steven Kramer and is explained in detail in their book *The Progress Principle: Using small wins to ignite joy, engagement, and creativity at work.* The progress principle shows us that the more frequently we experience a sense of progress on a big project, the more creatively productive we become. And one of the ways to reinforce this feeling of progress is to put in place a trigger called a *Nourisher*, which is external encouragement.

Now, hanging on to rejection letters—or today, to emails from agents not interested in our manuscript—may seem like a counter-productive act. Why in the world would we want to hold on to all of that negative feedback? Even letters that offer encouragement start to feel hollow after fifteen or twenty well-meaning comments like, "I love the voice of your writing, but..." or "Your story has great potential, but..."

When I received my 55th agent rejection—an email I'd waited three months to receive since that agent had requested my full manuscript and asked me to stop submitting to other agents since she felt confident about the story based on my first fifty pages—I wanted to take her "Sorry, but..." email and stick it in her sorry... never mind. I was upset.

But the truth is that there is success worth celebrating in those fifty-five agent rejections. It meant that I was brave fifty-five times. I had enough faith in my story and my characters' journeys to put that story into the world to be judged.

Beatrix Potter and Marcel Proust received so many rejections from publishers that they decided to self-publish their books way before self-publishing was even a thing. Those indie-published books became ones we all know and millions of readers have loved.

Your Turn

Since your brain is likely going to be a lying liar and remind you only of the days that writing was hard, of the paragraphs that were throw-aways, and of the times you sat down at the promised hour and were only able to type 32 words—you need to track all the days you had wins.

In fact, as you start building your writing routine, it's helpful to track a few different dimensions of your process. Overlapping these you may see patterns which could help you recognize that, for instance, you write best after you've had a glass of wine... or after yoga class... or are sitting in your car outside of your local coffee shop.

You can create your own spreadsheet or **download one from our creativeacademyforwriters.com/resources page.**

- In column 1, write the date.
- In column 2, write the time you sat down to work on your book.

- In column 3, write the time you stopped working on your book (time).
- In column 4, write the number of words you wrote (quantity).
- In column 5, use a scale that allows you to qualify how fun the writing was. For instance, a scale of 1 to 3 where 1 is easy/fun, 2 is a challenge, and 3 is like pulling teeth. (joy factor)
- In column 6, use a scale again to qualify how much you like the words you wrote. Be fair with yourself. If you wrote 150 words and have a lovely sentence or paragraph, give yourself full points. You have to remember that you are working on your scrappy rough draft, you're not writing the polished draft. (quality)
- An optional column 7 can be quite educational for those of us who tend to judge our first drafts harshly. If you can track which scene you've ranked in column 6, go back and read the scene after it's sat for a few days or weeks. You might very well find that the words you ranked on your scale as "meh," are actually pretty darned good.

The way you can use this chart to acknowledge small wins is really simple:

At the end of each writing sprint, take 30 seconds to fill in the blanks on your chart, then use a highlighter in a colour you love, to mark a win. It could be a win on one, two or even all four of the dimensions you're tracking.

For instance, if you had fun writing a conversation between your heroine and the bad guy, mark that block and give yourself a mental nod for having enjoyed the writing time. (the joy factor).

If you wrote more words in your focused time than you've written before, mark the quantity box and acknowledge the fact that you're getting faster. Odds are that you'll start to see that box marked off with more and more regularity as you outdo your previous best writing day. You are building your writer's muscle. Well done.

If you sat down to write for fifteen minutes and actually kept at it for thirty minutes, highlight your time box and give yourself a high-five for your commitment to getting this story told.

And then, tell a friend. Pick someone who you know will tell you how great you are, how proud they are of your commitment to your book, and how much they admire you.

And, if you can't think of anyone who fits the bill, who will be your writing cheerleader, visit our uber-supportive gang of peer authors in The Creative Academy. We've got your back.

22

BRINGING IT TOGETHER

In this book you've learned at least twenty different ways to use science to strategically motivate yourself and finish writing your book. If just one of the ideas resonated and gave you the push you need today to write tomorrow, that's a win. If a few ideas made you recognize and set aside old, ineffective ways of approaching your writing so that tomorrow, and tomorrow, and tomorrow, creeping along at this steady pace from day to day you get *all* the words of your own scrappy rough draft written—that would bring me the greatest joy.

If your scrappy rough draft happens to be part of a series, then I recommend you check out *Strategic Series Author: Plan, write and publish a series to maximize readership & income* by Crystal Hunt, as that will help you to spin the threads of this book, into many others.

I leave you with an affirmation, an homage to Anne Lamott. Make it your own by inserting your special word to positively describe your first draft. (If you're not sure what that your special word is, Chapter 1 will help you figure it out).

> *"Optimism is the voice of the first draft writer, the confident comrade of the creative. You will let it flourish and feed your whole manuscript. Optimism is the main touchstone between you and your <**your special word**> first draft." ~your name*

Or, if Chapter 5 helped you recognize that your most motivational inner voice speaks to you in the first person, this version:

> *"Optimism is the voice of the first draft writer, the confident comrade of the creative. I will let it flourish and feed my whole manuscript. Optimism is the main touchstone between me and my <**your special word**> first draft." ~your name*

The most important take-away from this book is that **you already have everything you need to finish your scrappy rough draft right inside you.** It's been there since the day you first decided to write a book. And it's there still. You simply need to see it and believe it.

I hope *Scrappy Rough Draft* has helped.

Your Turn

Exercise 1: Leave a review

I hope you found this book helpful. I'd be forever grateful if you took a moment right now to post a quick review wherever you bought your copy, and maybe also on Goodreads and BookBub if you have accounts there.

Your review will help other writers find the book, and in turn get their own scrappy rough drafts written.

It also helps me know what you found most helpful. This book is part of a series and your feedback will ensure our next books give you more of what you liked–so if you include that in your reviews we'll see it and take note!

Exercise 2: Share with a friend

The only thing better than writing and reading books is sharing books with friends. If you know other writers who are struggling with getting their scrappy rough drafts written, please let them know you enjoyed this one and found it helpful.

Exercise 3: Join our Mighty Network of Writers

Having a community who understand what you're going through as a writer makes all the difference between getting *stuck* or getting *done*. Join our fabulous free community at **creativeacademyforwriters.com/ community** and get access to a ton of resources.

Exercise 4: Check out the other books in this series

It's always sad when you come to the end of a book. But put away your Kleenex. We've got more books to help you along your writer journey. Be sure to check out our other titles in the *Creative Academy Guides for Writers* series and let us know what you think.

More Creative Academy Guides for Writers

We've got a whole series of books to help you along your writing and publishing journey.

Available in eBook & print!

Scrappy Rough Draft by Donna Barker
Build Better Characters by Eileen Cook
Strategic Series Author by Crystal Hunt
Create Story Conflict by Eileen Cook
Write Right Now by Donna Barker
Write More Books by Crystal Hunt

If you'd like an email notification each time we release a new title in this series, visit creativeacademyforwriters.com/books and get thee on our mailing list!

ACKNOWLEDGMENTS

This book would not have been written were it not for my dear friend, Nicole, who allowed me to host a DIY writer's retreat in her home in 2016. Only three of us participated, but the energy and ideas that we brainstormed that weekend were the genesis for creating The Creative Academy.

I am forever indebted to the conference organizers who've allowed me to test many of the ideas I share in this book in workshops. And of course, to all of the participants who've played along, given me feedback, and provided real life examples for many of the exercises.

To the writers who've trusted me as their coach—who've come to me with fear and frustrations about writing their personal stories and who have finished their scrappy rough drafts and gone on to pitch and publish—you are my inspiration to continue learning and to be more brave in my own writing and publishing.

My beta readers, Elissa, Marie, Deniz, Rena, Natasha, and Gay—wow! Your attention to detail and honesty when you thought I could do better made the last draft editing process an absolute joy. Five stars to each of you. (And consider yourself on-call for my next books in this series).

To all of the members of The Creative Academy who show up and do the work even when it's hard, who support each other (and me) as we celebrate successes and grumble about set-backs, and who are the freaking Gold Standard of community—you are the reason I brush my hair every morning.

And finally, my deepest love to my series co-authors, Eileen Cook and Crystal Hunt. Without your unwavering encouragement and witch-wizard support, *Scrappy Rough Draft* might still be a shitty first draft. My greatest wish is that every writer find their own version of an Eileen and a Crystal.

LIST OF RESOURCES

Bird by Bird: Some Instructions on Writing and Life by Anne Lamott, Anchor, 1995

Build Better Characters: The psychology of backstory & how to use it in your writing to hook readers by Eileen Cook, The Creative Academy, 2019

Conversations About Writing: Eavesdropping, Inkshedding and Joining In by Elizabeth Sargent, Sargent & Paraskevas, 2005

Decisive: How to Make Better Choices in Life and Work by Dan and Chip Heath, Random House, 2014

Great at Work: How Top Performers Work Less and Achieve More by Morten Hansen, Simon & Schuster, 2019

Let It Bleed: How to Write a Rockin' Memoir by Pamela De Barres, TarcherPerigee, 2017

Loving What Is: Four Questions That Can Change Your Life by Byron Katie, Three Rivers Press, 2003

Mindset: The New Psychology of Success by Carol Dweck, Ballantine Books, 2007

On Writing: A Memoir of the Craft by Stephen King, Sribner, Anniversary Edition, 2010

Procrastination and Blocking: A Novel, Practical Approach by Robert Boice, Praeger, 1996

Strategic Series Author: Plan, write and publish a series to maximize readership & income by Crystal Hunt, The Creative Academy, 2019

The Emotional Brain: The Mysterious Underpinnings of Emotional Life by Joseph LeDoux, Simon & Schuster, 2015

The Essential Don Murray: Lessons From America's Greatest Writing Teacher by Donald Murray, Heinemann, 2009

The Progress Principle: Using small wins to ignite joy, engagement, and creativity at work by Teresa Amabile & Steven Kramer, Harvard Business Review Press, 2011

The Writer's Book of Hope by Ralph Keyes, Holt Paperbacks, 2003

Wabi Sabi for Writers: Find Inspiration. Respect Imperfection. Create Peerless Beauty., by Richard R. Powell, Adams Media, 2006

Well Designed Life: 10 Lessons in Brain Science & Design Thinking for a Mindful, Healthy, & Purposeful Life by Kyra Bobinet, engagedIN Press, 2015

When a Writer Can't Write: Studies in Writer's Block and Other Composing Problems edited by Mike Rose, The Guilford Press, 1985

Writing Down the Bones: Freeing the Writer Within by Natalie Goldberg, Shambhala Publications, Anniversary edition, 2016

Writing From the Inside Out by Dennis Palumbo, Wiley, 2000

Made in the USA
San Bernardino, CA
19 July 2020